HOW TO MOVE UP WHEN THE ONLY WAY IS DOWN

LESSONS

FROM

ARTIFICIAL INTELLIGENCE

FOR

OVERCOMING YOUR LOCAL MAXIMUM

JUDAH TAUB

WILEY

Published by John Wiley & Sons, Inc., Hoboken, New Jersey.
Published simultaneously in Canada.

For general information on our other products and services or for technical support, please contact our Customer Care Department within the United States at (800) 762-2974, outside the United States at (317) 572-3993 or fax (317) 572-4002.

Wiley also publishes its books in a variety of electronic formats. Some content that appears in print may not be available in electronic formats. For more information about Wiley products, visit our website at www.wiley.com.

Library of Congress Cataloging-in-Publication Data:

Names: Taub, Judah, author.
Title: How to move up when the only way is down : lessons from artificial
    intelligence for overcoming your local maximum / Judah Taub.
Description: Hoboken, New Jersey : Wiley, [2025] | Includes index.
Identifiers: LCCN 2024020702 (print) | LCCN 2024020703 (ebook) | ISBN
    9781394278091 (hardback) | ISBN 9781394278084 (adobe pdf) | ISBN
    9781394278077 (epub)
Subjects: LCSH: Decision making. | Artificial intelligence.
Classification: LCC HD30.23 .T38 2025 (print) | LCC HD30.23 (ebook) | DDC
    658.4/03—dc23/eng/20240603
LC record available at https://lccn.loc.gov/2024020702
LC ebook record available at https://lccn.loc.gov/2024020703

Cover Design: Paul McCarthy
Cover Art: © Getty Images | Da-Kuk

To Aviad, Itamar, Lavi, and Meital, the lights of my life.

Contents

Foreword

Consider intelligence.

What do we mean by it, what forms does it take, where is it headed?

As we look to the future, the past speaks volumes. It is a story of ever-increasing intelligence. A story not devoid of challenge, strife, and opportunity.

The first age of intelligence – the age of biological intelligence – well predates humanity. Brimming with thought processes of many types and degrees, it is noteworthy that nature, too, is characterized by social organization and of rival parties advancing competing goals. Characteristic of this period is that intelligence at the organism (or collective) level is bound by its biological limits. These limits also govern the rate at which intelligence increases.

The second age of intelligence is the age of humanity and technological augmentation. As humans, we have transcended our biological limits. We have learned to harness technology to augment our capabilities and enhance our individual and collective intelligence at a snowballing rate. Our increased capabilities allow us, in turn, to further advance and evolve technology itself at an ever-accelerating rate. Thus far, our ever-more-capable technologies are developed in our service, with limited agency of their own.

We are now at the precipice of the third age of intelligence – the age of Artificial Intelligence (AI). In this epoch we will face radically new and diverse forms of intelligence. And for the first time, these intelligent agents will have evolving goals of their own. These intelligences can and will self-improve – unshackled by their corporal underpinnings. This is not a future of silicon alone; this is a future of rewriting biology as well. Most importantly, it is a future of nonhuman intelligence, far surpassing our own.

As I write these words, I am making my way to MIT, where I lead the FundamentalAI group within the MIT Futuretech project. On a daily basis we consider and push at these fundamental limits of AI, limits of both performance and safety. We are working toward ushering in this third epoch, such that *when, not if* AI exceeds human capabilities across any and all tasks, it does so in the service of humanity.

It is against this backdrop, of improving agents of artificial intelligence, that I find fascinating Judah's question of "What I, an intelligence bounded individual – and agent of natural augmented intelligence if you will – can learn and very practically adopt in improving myself by drawing on AI's mechanisms of improvement?"

In the quest for artificial intelligence, it has long been the case that our understanding of learning itself, the process by which we imbue intelligence with capabilities and skills, has looked inward to how humans and other organisms learn.

In building AI systems our understanding is being afforded newfound tools; as we can pry at the very inner workings of these systems as they learn and perform, we can change them and the way we teach them and assess the effects on their performance.

While our understanding of artificial intelligence learning and improvement remains remarkably opaque (even though we're the ones building these machines), we are already beginning to gain incredible insights.

Tapping into these insights, *How to Move Up When the Only Way Is Down* inverts the traditional question "What insights of human intelligence can we apply to improve AI?" and instead asks "What insights from AI improvement can we apply to improve ourselves?"

Core to the notion of improving is the concept of reaching the *best* possible solution, of reaching a *Global Maximum*, and avoiding the plethora of suboptimal solutions – *Local Maxima*. As alluded to by the title, Judah deeply engages and adopts this long-known concept in the fields of mathematics and computer science as a framework: explicitly, a framework of how to deal with the challenge of Local Maxima, where one reaches a peak where any further progress involves an initial regression.

This problem has applications in many fields of endeavor, professional and personal. It has also become a critical dilemma at the global level with implications across healthcare, global trade, the environment, and many other critical domains.

With a background in investing in technological innovation and in dealing with sensitive defense and intelligence issues, Judah is able to draw on a wide range of compelling examples to show how new AI-generated understandings can contribute to our own thinking on the most urgent and thorny issues. In doing so, he makes complex new ideas both digestible and easy to understand, and provides a valuable toolbox for moving up, even when the only way seems to be down.

More broadly, this book provides a model for a question that will increasingly accompany us in the years to come: Are lessons even transferable between artificial intelligence and human intelligence in addressing the challenges that we face? After all, unlike in the artificial case, I don't get to swap my computational hardware and am not afforded the parallelism of virtually limitless experiences or attempts.

How to Move Up When the Only Way Is Down suggests persuasively that lessons from AI are transferable with concrete practical implications. And so, while it may be the case that we are ushering in intelligence surpassing our own well before fully understanding either, it heartens me to consider that in so doing we may be finding ways to better ourselves and our society.

Enjoy the ride.

Dr. Jonathan ("Jonny") Rosenfeld
Co-Founder and CTO at Somite.ai
Head of FundamentalAI group at MIT FutureTech

Introduction: The Local Maximum Trap: A Universal Challenge

John's earliest memory is of playing with his father's stethoscope. He's always dreamed of following in his dad's footsteps and becoming a surgeon. Most of his college classes have been pre-med, but, by the end of sophomore year, he's felt a pull toward biomedical engineering. His academic advisor has been encouraging him to specialize (his father has, too), and it's time to declare a major. John's not positive which career path will lead to the best outcome. His dad's surgical residency has led to a very nice life for the family, but he wonders if he can make a greater impact on people's lives from the engineering side. Part of the dilemma is that he's still learning and gathering information. He's not sure he has enough to go on to decide, but the registrar needs an answer.

Lucy has been playing the dating game for 15 years, and she's eager to get married and start a family. She's dated over 80 guys;

1

three of which were serious. She wonders, is she being too picky, or was one of those three the "one"? Should she stay in the dating pool and keep looking for her dream partner, or should she let go of some of the "must haves" in lieu of what "will do"?

Fred is a top-level marketing executive with a high salary and lifestyle expenses to match. From the outside, his life seems enviable. He's been on a steady career trajectory for 15 years, gathering prestige and properties along the way. But when he thinks about how he really wants to spend his time, marketing is not it. The problem is his salary is so high, he'll have to take a severe loss to go in a different direction. He's trapped in the proverbial golden handcuffs.

John, Lucy, and Fred are each stuck in a Local Maximum. In nearly every field of human endeavor and facet of decision-making, in which we aim to go as high as possible, a Local Maximum is a point from which we can only go down. Crucially, we may not be at the highest point. There are higher peaks around us, but we find ourselves trapped on our own peak within our own Local Maximum, with significant costs and implications, but without the necessary tools, or even the language, to describe them.

Though humans may lack the nomenclature to articulate their predicaments (beyond the word, "stuck"), there are several cutting-edge industries in which the challenge of Local Maximum is well-known. And because of the enormous costs it can incur, it has been given careful attention. These include fusing alloys, telecom routing, weather forecasting, mobile advertising, oil and gas mining, molecular modeling, aerodynamics, cryptography, and many more. They are encountered by the brightest coders and engineers at tech giants like Google and Amazon.[1] Professionals within these arenas readily acknowledge that getting stuck with suboptimal solutions is one of the biggest issues they face. Critically, the challenge of a Local Maximum is not exclusive to the tech industry, to computer scientists, or to programmers. The challenge exists in ways both large and small, personally and professionally, for everyone, as evidenced by John, Lucy, and Fred.

In my own life, the concept of Local Maximum has crept in through the back door and become a key factor in determining an initiative's success or failure. As an intelligence officer in national security, I have been trained to think in new and innovative ways to reverse engineer my regiment's way out of both common and uncommon military challenges: how to analyze the field, how to define its parameters, and how to tackle complex problems effectively and efficiently under duress. In my career first at a hedge fund and then as co-founder and managing partner of Hetz Ventures, an international investment fund focused on early stage Israeli start-ups led by hi-tech entrepreneurs, and as a board member of many of those companies, I have the opportunity to help founders identify and avoid Local Maximums every day. The CEOs of these companies are dealing with hundreds of oversight-related items, very few of which have to do with actual innovation, strategy, or implementation (or, not nearly as much as they would like). They are focused on the nuts and bolts of daily operations, so when we sit down to talk, they're craving a high-level perspective as to whether their efforts, or the organization's efforts, are driving them to the optimal outcome. They want to know: Are we climbing toward the highest point? In these two very different environments, my military colleagues and the start-up entrepreneurs are amongst the most talented, driven, educated, and thoughtful people in their fields. But it turns out, running as fast as you can toward the highest point is not always the best strategy.

How to Navigate This Book

For decades, since the advent of computer programming, talented programmers have used their best efforts to teach computers human logic. A classic example is – if A is bigger than B, and B is bigger than C, then A must be bigger than C. In recent years, though, computers have begun to develop a logic of their own. This book turns the tables and asks what we humans can now learn from how computers make decisions. Specifically, it focuses on the challenge of avoiding the Local Maximum trap. Now that the brightest minds of tech giants such as Amazon and Google have devoted years to addressing this challenge and saving billions of dollars and millions of work-hours, this book explores what computers can teach us about avoiding the Local Maximum trap in our own lives.

Rest assured this book does NOT require a background in computing, engineering, or math. In fact, as you will see, the major obstacles we face emerge from human psychology far more than from algorithms. At the end of each chapter, I have included a short section titled "A Little Byte of Data Science," which you should feel fine to skip. Although they do not require knowledge of, or interest in, technology, they demonstrate how the ideas from each chapter are used in the tech world.

In Chapter 1, we explore the concept of Local Maximum through the metaphor of a combat paratrooper in training. He is dropped into the middle of the desert and given the task of climbing the tallest mountain. How does he decide which mountain to climb, and how does he know it is the tallest? Through his experience searching for a solution to a seemingly simple problem, we will see that Local Maximum is a challenge with far-reaching implications and applications.

In Chapter 2, we focus on understanding why Local Maximums can be so attractive and the dangers of the most common methods used by marketers, strategic planners, and others to assess potential courses of action. We will learn the extraordinary and simple power of tweaking our thinking and metrics by moving from A/B testing to A/B/X testing.

In Chapter 3, we ask how we can get off a Local Maximum when we find ourselves stranded on one. We will analyze "death valleys" – the seemingly insurmountable canyons between where we are and where we need to be. And we will encounter practical examples from fields as diverse as Military Intelligence to career choices of Ethiopians living in Israel to international Judo competitions.

In Chapter 4, we turn inward and understand how certain personal or organizational characteristics make us more susceptible to falling foul of a Local Maximum. We will consider how we can develop practices, such as balancing agility and muscle, to achieve our current targets while reducing the potential pain of hitting a Local Maximum.

In Chapter 5, we address the psychological dimension and contrast the Local Maximum mindset with a Global Maximum way of thinking. With lessons from the Israeli Air Force and the future of Healthcare 3.0, we'll see that often our greatest mental strengths can also be our most forceful opponent.

In Chapter 6, we discover that time can both constrain and expand our realm of possible outcomes. We learn to view time as a variable rather than a fixed factor, and − like YouTube, drone units, and early-stage start-ups − utilize this knowledge to our advantage.

In Chapter 7, we dig down into our core values and consider how the degree to which we see ourselves, as individuals or as part of a collective, impacts our ability to overcome obstacles and reach higher ground. Charles Darwin, Robin Dunbar, and the Joker from *Batman* may believe our DNA limits our potential, but ants may suggest otherwise.

In Chapter 8, we consider not only the height of the mountain we are aiming to climb, but its unique shape. We will learn to recognize the topography of different types of dangerous mountains. With examples from hedge fund managers and public company CEOs, greatest of all-time (GOAT) athletes and major start-up busts, we will meet four mountain shapes to be wary of.

In Chapter 9, we pause to consider whether there may be situations in which a Local Maximum is not a bug, but actually something to aim for. Wildfires, viruses, and US sports leagues all offer unique insights to utilizing the tools from earlier chapters to our advantage.

Finally, in Chapter 10, we put the lessons we've learned from artificial intelligence to the test by examining five fundamental global challenges. We examine whether the tools we have acquired can provide a fresh look at education, globalization, governance, healthcare, and technological development.

How to Move Up When the Only Way Is Down: Lessons from Artificial Intelligence for Overcoming Your Local Maximum is a tool to observe problems in a new way, and it is a mechanism to monitor the long-term health of an individual, corporate, or societal trajectory. To harness the full impact of the concept, we will explore the numerous techniques, typically taken from the computing world, to recognize, solve for, and avoid a Local Maximum. Though we are not all computer programmers, we are Johns, Lucys, and Freds, looking for tools to help guide us in the hardest decisions we have to make.

Chapter 1

The Highest Mountain

We have lost the battle, but we won the war.
— Pyrrhus of Epirus, Battle of Asculum (279 BCE)

Imagine you have just been dropped from a helicopter into the middle of the Negev Desert. Four other soldiers from your battalion have been dropped at different points and are nowhere in sight.

Your mission: Locate the *highest* peak within 10 square miles and be the first of the group to climb to the top. You have 12 hours to get there.

This is the toughest test in your combat paratrooper training so far. You're well beyond communications satellite range, you have no navigational tools, and you're surrounded by dusty sand dunes and jagged mountain ranges as far as the eye can see. In the vast desolation, the wind whistles as you get situated and visually zero in on what appears to be the tallest mountain in sight. Adjusting your pack, heavy with enough water and rations for the day, you start toward the base.

After three hours of battling heavy, dry sand, you reach the base of the mountain range, well ahead of the other guys. Preparing to begin the ascent, you're aware of your buddy, Yoni, in the distance, gaining traction and proximity, but you've got the lead. Your blood is pumping with adrenaline, knowing Yoni always has an energetic reserve tank, and you have to widen the gap. Recalling that half the guys from last week's exercise didn't make it to the top of the mountain, and your friend Daniel was hospitalized overnight from exertion, you pick up speed. There's no way you're going to be in the 20% of aspiring troopers cut from the program. Not today. No way.

The climb entails steep switchbacks, navigating around and over boulders and slippery sand dunes, and ripping through spiky cactus trees. After three more hours of grueling effort, you pause briefly to dump the rocks out of your boots, refuel, rehydrate, and reassess.

The last time you spotted Yoni was an hour ago, when he abruptly veered inward off the "trail" and vanished out of sight, seemingly heading toward a smaller mountain. What does he know? Where did he go? You haven't seen a glimpse or heard so much as a twig snap from the other three soldiers. Where could they be? You're too close to the top to worry about them. They'll figure it out. Or perhaps they won't.

With renewed determination, you push upward, satisfied knowing you're in the lead and making good time. At this pace, you calculate, you could conceivably summit within an hour. You tap into your own energy reserve tank and break into a run.

By late afternoon, you've reached the peak, physically and mentally exhausted. Taking in a long, deep breath of fresh mountain air, what the troops call the "victory inhale," you ease your pack to the ground and sit down on a smooth, flat rock to remove your boots and rub your blisters. You executed this drill to perfection: at every decision point you made the right decision, successfully detouring around a few smaller mountains, keeping up pace, and then, using the last of your energy to race up the final incline.

Slowly, draining the last of the water from your canteen, you settle in to wait for Yoni and the others to catch up. Raising your eyes, you take in the magnificent clarity of the distant mountain range that surrounds the one you're on – the one you've conquered, and with time to spare.

Just then, a heavy feeling lands in the pit of your stomach and slowly travels through your pulsing bloodstream up to your head. Doubt spreads through every rational thought as it dawns on you, with absolute certainty, something is terribly wrong. Where are the others? They should be here by now, or at least within earshot. Either they miscalculated, or you did.

Rising to walk to the edge of the very peak you climbed, you're gob-smacked at what you see. There is another mountain, right in front of you, and it's taller than the one you're on. You're on the wrong mountain.

You release a pained and violent wail into the open air. It taunts back in a cold and rippling echo.

Your mind races: "No. This is impossible. What the hell? How?"

You did everything right! You did not set out haphazardly. You made a plan, calculated the distance within the allotted time, conserved your energy and your rations, and made admirable advances despite the obstacles.

Peering down, you can just barely make out the shape of another climber at the bottom of the tallest mountain beginning the ascent. It's that joker, Yoni! You are higher up than he is, but he is undeniably further ahead on the mission, because he is climbing *the tallest peak*. Every one of your steps up this mountain was a step further away from the peak you needed to reach. You got to the "top" and discovered that the only way forward is to go all the way back down.

You're at a Local Maximum, and the worst part – worse than all the time and energy you've already wasted, and worse than all that still lies ahead – is it could have been avoided. Even though you tried your very best and calculated every step along the way, you lost.

The painful realization that we have been investing our time, resources, and efforts to reach the wrong goal is one that can haunt us in many of the most important aspects of our lives.

Local Maximum: What It Is and Why It Matters

A Local Maximum is a point on a field that is not the highest or the best, but it is a point from which we can only go down. It's deceptive because it's attractive. We are naturally pulled toward it and work very hard to get there, but once we arrive, we realize there is a higher or better option.

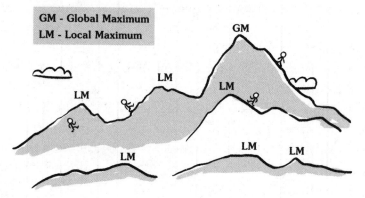

The terrain includes many maximum points from which a climber can only go down. There is one Global Maximum and many Local Maximums, some of which are very low down, but are nevertheless maximum points.

Most of us don't spend our lives in army fatigues navigating desert landscapes. But the Local Maximum scenario is one that affects us all, and in the most important aspects of our lives. As individuals, as managers, or as leaders, we devote our days, our skills, and our resources to pursuing particular goals. Yet, we are often blind as to whether a better, perhaps vastly better, course of action is available. We are so busy exercising our muscles to improve the speed and efficiency of our climb. But how effective are we at recognizing whether we are climbing the right peak in the first place, or in getting off the wrong peak to course correct while there is still time?

Consider the following real-life scenarios:

1. **The manager of an English football team at the bottom of the second division.**

    All the team players are average except for the star striker, who is responsible for most of the team's goals. The fact that all the other players are centered around the star player seriously limits their play and their own development. In the long run, the team would be better off without the star player. In the short term, there is a price to be paid: the team will likely go down a division, and it could take years to recover.

2. **The military needs to determine how to spend their budget.**

    Combat divisions need ammunition and motor vehicles, and they need to invest in intelligence to predict the type of warfare anticipated. How do you trade off building the military force (running up the mountain) while also balancing intelligence to make sure you are investing in the appropriate tools and training (heading in the right direction)?

3. **The CEO of a successful start-up that has gained tremendous traction.**

    Out of the gate and on a shoestring budget, the CEO introduced an immediately popular and widely adopted freemium product, generally known to be the envy of his heavily backed competitors. However, she needs to raise more money to bring the product to a broader market. Some investors are advising her to prioritize short-term revenues, which means sacrificing part of her unique brand and potentially alienating her original community of supporters.

4. **A senior government official charged with upgrading national infrastructure.**

    New 5G telecom technology promises major benefits throughout the country's economy. While it is clear 6G and 7G technologies will arise in the future and may render the enormously expensive investments in 5G redundant before too long, voters are hungry for speedy results. How do you balance the huge potential without getting stuck with a huge "sunk cost"?

Local Maximum offers a simple framework to understand why some businesses plateau, why some people find themselves in jobs they can't leave, and why we find ourselves trapped in situations that prevent us reaching our full potential in so many fields of life. Understanding this concept gives us the tools to ask:

- What are the behaviors or decisions that lead us to a Local Maximum?
- What can we do to steer ourselves away from these limiting Maximums before we get there?
- And, if we do get there, what can we do to get unstuck?

A Prime Example: The Delivery Route

A classic example of the Local Maximum challenge is Amazon Prime and its complex system to manage deliveries. Consider how the system determines the most efficient route for the driver to deliver packages to hundreds of locations around a city. This may sound like a simple A to B mapping project, but finding the optimal solution is nearly impossible due to the sheer volume of options.

Think about it this way. Imagine you need to make 10 deliveries across the city in a day. How many possible optimal routes are there? (The answer is over 3 million!) Now, pretend you have to make 20 deliveries, that is 3×10^{64} optional routes. (That's more than the number of steps it would take to "walk" to the Sun!) In reality, Amazon has thousands of drivers, and each of them make hundreds of deliveries a day; the number of route options is simply too large for the mind to comprehend. More so – and this might come as a surprise – the number of route options is too large for even the fastest and best computer to comprehend. So, how do computer scientists overcome this? They turn the problem into mountains.

So, consider Amazon Prime as a mountain climber:

Amazon Prime delivers packages. Its profit relates directly to the speed of its deliveries. The more deliveries it can make in an hour, the more profit. The process of planning delivery routes is a mountain that must be climbed. To solve the task, the data scientist converts the deliveries into a topographic map: the better the delivery route, the higher the point it represents on the map. (Routes that are similar appear next to each other.) Next, the data scientist asks himself: How do I reach the route/peak of greatest efficiency and avoid the costs of adopting a route/peak that looks efficient, but that ignores faster, more cost-effective routes/peaks?

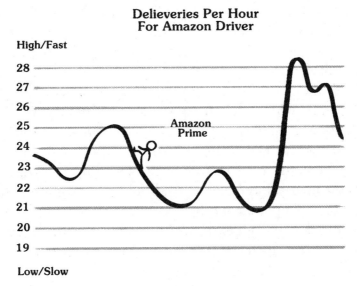

**Delieveries Per Hour
For Amazon Driver**

The Amazon Prime solution, represented by the figure, as if on a desert field. Each point on the field is a different potential solution, with the height representing the number of deliveries per hour the driver can make at that point. Notice how there are points where the algorithm can't improve with only one simple step, such as the 25 deliveries per hour point the current Amazon algorithm is heading toward. Hence, they are Local Maximums the system may return as the suggested solution.

Amazon Prime, and many other businesses, have spent huge sums of money and dedicated their brightest minds to develop solutions and new logics to alleviate the challenge of a Local Maximum.

Until recently, humans have not had the tools to address such dilemmas, or to even think about them effectively. But now that billions of dollars have been poured into improving computers' abilities to limit those effects, it is time for us humans to leverage these learnings so that we, too, can both identify Local Maximums and limit their negative impacts in our personal and professional lives.

Most decisions include an element of Local Maximum, and the more complex the decision, the stronger the effects and dangers of a Local Maximum. This concept can apply to decisions that have small effects, such as which ice cream flavor to choose or which shoes to buy, and to decisions that have very large effects, such as which job to pursue, how to help people out of extreme poverty, how to build a company's business roadmap, or even how to reach a carbon neutral society. The concept of Local Maximum offers new ways of thinking about human challenges as well as ways to avoid or address those problems, whether it's global warming or what to order for breakfast.

My work with start-ups and various other life experiences with Local Maximums has helped me to understand we are all in the desert on our personal or corporate journeys, like our paratrooper in training at the top of this chapter, trying to navigate our way to the highest mountaintop. Many times, we know we are not climbing the right mountain, but we are concerned about the costs of going back down. Other times, we may not be aware there is a much better mountain right around the corner. We need to understand our terrain to navigate it most effectively.

A Little Byte of Data Science

The idea of a Local Maximum comes from data science and mathematics, where the same concept is actually called a Local Minimum. The goal in data science is to find solutions that lead to a Global Minimum because engineers, mathematicians, and software developers want to do things in the shortest, quickest, most efficient manner. For example: What is the least amount of computing power required? How can we solve this problem in the least number of steps? Typically, the best solutions are represented by the least amount of energy, power, or data necessary to achieve the objective. All of the ideas in this book have been flipped from minimum to maximum to apply to human factors vs. technology factors. Humans are searching for the best and highest points. Data scientists are searching for the lowest possible points. Both terms – Local Maximum and Local Minimum – refer to the suboptimal outcome and are exactly the same.

The challenge of Local Minimum (or, in our terminology, Local Maximum) costs technology companies billions of dollars. So, in the case of Amazon Prime trying to deliver packages in the most efficient manner, an algorithm is constantly searching for a driver's optimal delivery route. The average Amazon Prime driver delivers to between 10 and 15 locations an hour, and the company makes roughly three and half million deliveries a day. Factor in the driver's hourly wage, the cost of gas and tolls, and even just a tiny increase in the algorithm's efficiency will save the company vast amounts of money, not to mention other benefits such as decreased pollution through less fuel consumption, less traffic on the road, and potential other benefits.

This is but one example of how computers try to solve for the problem of Local Minimum (which I call Local Maximum). Throughout the book, each chapter will conclude with a small data byte such as this to demonstrate how AI attempts to solve for specific, Local Maximum–related challenges so that we humans can learn to implement the same optimization tactics in our own lives.

Chapter 2

Assessing the Terrain vs. Climbing

Excellence is not a formula. Excellence is the grand experiment. It ain't mathematics. It's jazz.
— Dan Wieden, Creator of Nike's "Just Do It" (1988)

In October 1968, 21-year-old Dick Fosbury, a self-proclaimed awkward and uncoordinated engineering student from Oregon State University, traveled to Mexico City with the US Olympic team to compete in the high jump competition. No one — not his coach, his parents, or his teammates — could have predicted he would leave a permanent mark on the field of Athletics. A contender, but far from a favorite, he wasn't naturally skilled in the sport. Yet, at the packed Estadio Olimpico Universitario, Dick Fosbury "turned the event upside down"[1] and set a new world record. Now widely considered one of the most influential jumpers in the history of track and field, he used the occasion to debut his immediately famous "Fosbury Flop." Dick didn't set out to forever change the event; he just wanted to get over the bar.

During training, back in high school, Fosbury recalls he "gravitated toward the oldest style in high jump history, the scissors, but people didn't use it anymore. Everyone was using either the straddle or the Western roll," a technique that involved "vigorously kicking the lead leg" up over the bar.[2] The trailing leg then swung up to meet it as the body contorted, head facing the ground, for a three-point landing with both legs and hands.

Fosbury knew he was terrible at the scissors, the straddle, *and* the Western roll, though he and his teammates practiced dutifully, working steadily toward incremental improvements. The goal was to consistently jump just a tiny bit higher, to exceed their personal records, and to stay within the rules and boundaries of the game. The gains were marginal, and the critics on the sidelines were fierce. He remembers, "There were always a million experts to tell you why what you were doing was wrong."

Making minimal strides was the improvement strategy high jumpers had employed since the dawn of the sport: centimeter by measured centimeter. Like everyone else, Fosbury worked tirelessly to get better at the tried-and-true techniques. Someone documented his many efforts using old, black-and-white, 35 millimeter film. Anyone who chooses to Google him can easily find footage from his early high school and college training days, practicing the scissor versus the straddle, back and forth, back and forth, slowly getting a shred better each time.

Fosbury recognized incremental improvements weren't making a hill of a difference in his rankings. He needed to change how he jumped if he was going to keep up with the others and stay on the team. At home, at night, after another humiliating day at practice, still sweaty from exertion, he thought, "There's just got to be a better way. Something new. Something totally different that no one's ever thought of or seen before."

Fosbury was an engineer in training, after all. He had a logical mind and a natural, insatiable curiosity about how things were designed, created, and enhanced. He attacked his performance on the track like a scientific problem that needed to be solved. He studied books on high jumping improvement, mental preparedness in sports, physical stamina, and endurance; he collected and analyzed data about his every move, making minor tweaks here and there to gain a centimeter or two; he sketched diagrams of multiple scenarios and crunched mathematical equations factoring in speed, weight, and the laws of gravity. Rather than looking for incremental gains, he was looking for something that would change the entire playing field, even if it didn't allow him to jump higher straight away. He needed a solution that could potentially lead to jumping significantly higher, not just an incremental inch or two.

Early into Fosbury's high school career, high jumpers landed in pits built from hard sand or sawdust. In the early 1960s, a key modification occurred on the terrain. The once-hard sand pits were replaced with softer, deeper foam matting, which paved the way for new jumping and landing styles. The field was ripe for invention.

Fosbury was working toward his goal in a different way than everyone else. Unlike the other kids on his team, who spent most of their time striving for their next incremental gain, focusing down on a single improvement, and iterating from it, Fosbury wanted to be miles ahead – literal leaps and bounds – than the rest. He pushed himself by experimenting – using dramatic, never-before-seen-or-attempted variances in approaches, take offs, contortions, and landings.

Eventually, and utilizing the laws of physics in terms of speed and velocity, Fosbury "landed" (awkwardly) on a method that allowed him to smash his own record and achieve a significant height gain: from 5 feet to 6 feet, 7 inches. He gained over a foot and a half by employing a mid-air rotation, turning his back to the bar, instead of approaching it head-on, and landing backward on his head; a move that would not have been feasible if:

1. The landing terrain had not recently been changed to foam, and critically,
2. Fosbury had not attempted such a daring and dangerous new move.

He took his "discovery" and ran with it. "The advantage," Fosbury said, "from a physics standpoint is, it allows the jumper to run at the bar with more speed and, with the arch in your back, you could actually clear the bar and keep your center of gravity at or below the bar, so it was much more efficient."

"The Fosbury Flop" was born, and though it "looked like a guy falling off the back of a truck," according to one journalist, its effectiveness and originality were undisputed. Fosbury's unorthodox technique earned him the gold medal in the Mexico City 1968 Olympics with an unprecedented jump of 7 feet 4 ¼ inches. It also earned him the attention of the world and forever revolutionized the sport.

Following his groundbreaking performance, "The Fosbury Flop" became the dominant "gold standard" competitive style in the high jump. He wasn't the *best* jumper, and if everyone had been climbing the *same* mountain, he would never have won. He won the gold because he had the ingenuity to look for a better and higher mountain to climb, while everyone else was stuck at a Local Maximum on another mountain. In a world of incremental improvement, Dick Fosbury broke the mold.

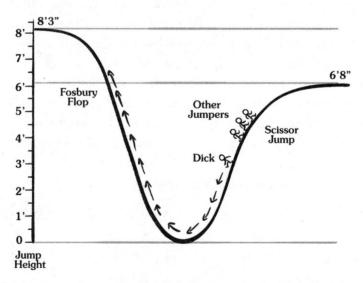

See the jumpers who are better than Dick gradually improve their scissor technique and jump higher. Dick can't keep up with them but realizes there is a better technique, the Flop. He eventually beats them using this technique. Years later, others break his record, obviously using the Flop rather than the Scissor Jump.

The Fosbury Flop is a visual and lasting example of how the concept of a Local Maximum and its limitations can be applied to real-world situations. Fosbury's initiative, his willingness to iterate and experiment for the best solution, to explore something totally unheard of, and to teach himself how to master it, is a testament to the power of innovation.

Just Do It: The Power of X

A/B (or split) testing is utilized across a variety of industries, including Marketing, Advertising, Product Development, and Machine Learning, generally with great success. In its basic form, it compares two versions of a variable, with a minuscule difference, to achieve an optimal outcome. Billions of dollars are poured into A/B testing every year because it's effective and, most importantly, improvements are visible every step of the way.

The advertising field is rich in examples of A/B tested slogans, but it's the Xs we remember. Certain catchphrases are so ground-breaking at their inception, they've become deeply ingrained in the cultural lexicon. The undisputed King of Catchy Advertising Slogans, and one that effectively created an empire, is "Just Do It." Its selling power has been "just doing it" for Nike since 1987.

Nike was Dan Wieden's very first client at his new advertising firm. In a previous life, Wieden had launched successful campaigns for name brands at the veteran ad agency McCann-Erikson: Old Spice, Coca-Cola, and Procter & Gamble among them. When Nike's co-founder, Phil Knight, came knocking in 1982, the company was just a small regional sportswear brand, and it was in a slump. It was losing market share and status to the aerobics fitness shoe brand, Reebok. Not long after the relationship began, Wieden came up with the slogan that "shifted design, innovation, and the ethos of advertising."[3] It also launched Nike into a major brand.

"Just Do It" was originally conceived as a tagline to offer cohesiveness for multiple product lines, a way to tie them all together under one umbrella. As Wieden tells it, he and his team had been working with Nike to launch their first major television campaign, and they were getting ready to roll out five separate commercials across internal brand departments: running, walking, cross-training, basketball, and women's fitness. A different creative team had devised each of the five commercials. When Wieden sat down to review the work the night before the big presentation to Nike, he felt "we needed a tagline to give some unity to the work, one that spoke to the hardest of hard-core athletes as well as those talking up a morning walk."[4]

The origin story of Nike's iconic slogan came from an unlikely and macabre inspiration. The words were lifted, in part, from convicted double murderer Gary Gilmore before he was executed via firing squad in 1977. When asked if he had any last words, he said, "Let's do it." Wieden was impressed, not by Gilmore's crimes, but by the "ultimate statement of intention,"[5] as recalled by Liz Dolan, former chief marketing officer at Nike, and the words stuck.

Many years later, when Wieden was preparing for the Nike five-tiered television commercial campaign, he recalled Gilmore's directive. Wieden swapped out Gilmore's "*Let's* do it" for "*Just* Do It" and took his "X" idea to Nike. They hated it. They said they didn't need it. In fact, Phil Knight brushed it off as "irrelevant." People from within Wieden's own team felt the same way. They just didn't get "it."

Wieden's response was, "Listen, I'm not married to it but let's test it in the market and if it doesn't work, we can drop it on the next round." Everyone shrugged and rolled their eyes. "Why not? What harm can it do?" they rationalized. Wieden said, "Just trust me on this one, give it a try," and thankfully for them (and their shareholders), they did.

The consumer response was deafening. "Immediately Nike started getting letters and phone calls, and so did Wieden & Kennedy. For some reason, 'Just Do It' resonated deeply in the athletic community and just as deeply with people who had little or no connection to sports. For some, it became a doctrine to live by."[6]

Wieden's unplanned, last-minute, umbrella tagline was a powerful rallying call and an inspirational directive that seeped into the fabric of the culture. It shattered limiting category labels (sportswear!) and made the company accessible to a broader, global audience, all without mentioning the name of the company or what it sells.

Wieden put Nike on a different mountain. He was the Dick Fosbury of the advertising world. Almost overnight, Nike became a major international fashion brand, leaving the sportswear category in the dust and changing what was possible in the advertising realm.

Dusting Off an Old Invention

X doesn't always have to be something entirely new. Our constant search for progress, or for the new thing, might blind us to the fact that X could be something we have already considered but discarded or abandoned.

When COVID first appeared in Wuhan, China, in late 2019, the necessity for ventilators to save lives became immediately apparent. When the virus spread and surged in Italy, Spain, the United States, and the UK, that need became dire. Healthcare systems strained and governments scrambled to accommodate the ventilator shortage, while news reports showed people lined up on cots in the streets, desperately awaiting critical respiratory care. Within a two-and-a-half-week time span, every country in the world was looking for ventilators.

The leading ventilator was made by Dräger in Germany and cost about $50,000 each. In Israel, we immediately placed an order, but as demand grew, the price quickly jumped up to $150,000. Even at such a ridiculous price, the government approved the purchase. Three days later, Germany decided no ventilators were to leave the country, no matter how much money was paid upfront. And Israel, like many other countries, was suddenly faced with the question: What can we manufacture internally and how quickly?

Before I knew it, I was part of a think tank team to solve the ventilator problem and save lives. Frantic leading military personnel, doctors, and engineers started throwing out ideas. How could we replicate Dräger's ventilator technology? What parts of their machine were absolutely necessary, and what could we do without? How could we work backwards to strip away the excess features and identify only the most essential components?

After two days of brainstorming with the greatest minds in the country, I received a phone call from my Great Uncle Joey. Now, Uncle Joey is an interesting character. He was the first person in my family to move to Israel at the age of 18. Legend has it, he drove a moped all the way from England, which is a damn long journey, let alone on two wheels. Upon arrival, he joined the Air Force and eventually became one of the country's leading cardiac surgeons. He's always been known in my family as the guy with magic hands who can build just about anything, including a backyard Jacuzzi, an airplane, and – as luck would have it – a ventilator. Turns out, the military asked him to build one back in the 1990s in the event of a chemical warfare attack, and he had the thing sitting in his garage, covered in 30 years' worth of dust.

Lo and behold, in our darkest hour, my 80-year-old Uncle Joey's dusty old clunker of a rudimentary ventilator worked! And the reason it worked is because it was so simple and so basic (it only had one moving part). It turned out to be more robust and functional than the Germans' sophisticated, complex, unaffordable, and unavailable ventilator. When we dug up the military's requirements for the project, we discovered they only asked that Uncle Joey's invention should hold up if it was hit by a bus. Not only could his ventilator withstand a forceful impact, it could also ventilate multiple people in parallel, and it only cost $400 to produce.

Three weeks later, we had a working ventilator based on Uncle Joey's model. It turned out that going back to his old and primitive prototype was more effective and efficient than anything new or repurposed the think tank team or the Germans had devised. Thankfully, Israel didn't end up needing as many ventilators as anticipated, but it was deeply comforting to know that our X was safely stowed away in Uncle Joey's garage.

Testing, Testing: A/B/X

The power of X is undeniable, but A/B testing has a huge number of advantages. It's easy to use, and you can see your improvement with every step you take. If you are a manager tasked with executing a multi-million-dollar budget, A/B testing will yield both data and a respectable result. A/B testing, however, has one obvious flaw: it's almost certain to end in a Local Maximum – one that could be significantly worse than a different solution, and you, your team, and whoever else is involved will never know.

So, how can we be more like Fosbury, Just Do It, and my Great Uncle Joey? We cannot randomly try different ideas, without a strategy, and hope to stumble upon our lucky, million-dollar X. That approach would never fly.

To introduce X into our thinking, we need to answer two questions. First, how often should we disrupt our standard A/B approach by introducing an outlier option? Second, how much of an outlier should this option actually be? The answers to these questions depend on a large range of factors, many of them specific to particular fields, but still, a number of guiding questions can act as guardrails for our thinking.

First, ask yourself, how confident are you in understanding your surrounding terrain? The more confident you are, the less Xs you may need. Next, test where you currently stand in relation to your mission. Similarly, with the distance from your target, the further you are away, the more value there may be in checking out more off-the-wall approaches. Finally, when choosing an X, prioritize the one likely to have the biggest impact on your current thinking, otherwise it is probably another A/B rather than a genuinely different approach.

Elon Musk is a master of X thinking, and he is obsessed with the letter X. His spacecraft manufacturing company is called

SpaceX, he renamed Twitter "X," and he even named one of his children X Æ. He often forgoes a typical A/B approach and leaps straight to a potential X.

For example, in contrast to NASA, which continually looked to improve its space rockets in a repetitive manner, SpaceX announced its goal out of the gate was to reduce rocket-launching costs by 98%. This approach eliminated standard A/B gains and forced the company to think in big X-style leaps, including unheard of practices such as returning rockets they'd launched back to Earth and reusing them.

Musk's X-thinking was on full display when he purchased Twitter. The company's original vision was to "reach the largest daily audience in the world by connecting everyone. . . ." Since he took over and transitioned it to X, the new stated vision is to be the "App for Everything." Another of his endeavors, The Boring Company, doesn't try to improve travel infrastructure through faster cars or better roads, but by constructing a network of tunnels for hyperloop travel. It's unclear whether these ideas will materialize successfully or not. But as Musk said, "Failure is an option. However, if you are not failing, you are not innovating." For him, innovating means looking for X.

How Much Is Night Vision Worth?

Let's revisit our paratrooper scenario from the previous chapter. Put yourself back in the Negev Desert, trying to get to the tallest peak before anyone else in the platoon. You're climbing and climbing in the dead of night, and it's pitch black all around you. You can't see more than 10 meters ahead or behind. You know you are moving up, but it's a complete guess as to whether you're on the right mountain.

Are you willing to trade 30 minutes of mobility in return for a few glimpses through a pair of night vision goggles?

Of course, your answer will depend on a variety of factors, such as how much more time you have to get to the top of the mountain. If you only have 40 minutes left for the climb, the sacrifice is not worth it. But, if you have another 10 hours to go, sacrificing 30 minutes of mobility in return for visual clarity would be worth it. You might also want to know how powerful the goggles are. How far into the darkness will they allow you to see and with what specificity? Night vision goggles could provide numerous valuable advantages under the right conditions.

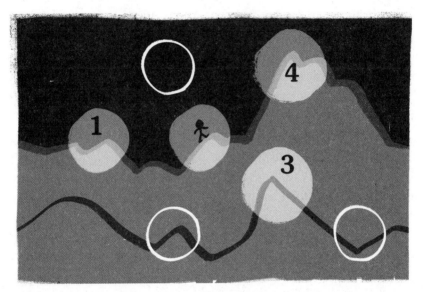

The climber in the dark can only see a small radius around himself. He chooses to point his night vision goggles in three directions, where he believes the information will impact him the most. In this diagram, it is intuitive to choose the highlighted circles rather than the white rims. In everyday decisions, we must learn to use our Xs wisely, too.

In the A/B/X testing model, X is often the glimpses through night vision goggles. You may learn you need more time with the goggles and sacrifice another 30 minutes of mobility, or you may learn you can put them away and confidently double down on your current path.

Regardless of whether you decide to add an X to every five, ten, or one hundred A/B cycles, adding X for A/B/X testing is critical. It allows for your inner Fosbury to fight the urge to run toward the nearest peak and claim a small victory.

R&D: Scouts vs. Climbers

Despite the commonality of combining Research and Development in corporate structures, countries, productivity analysis, and many other realms, "R & D" are vastly different functions and should be treated as such. Personally, it drives me nuts to see these two functionalities combined on every tax return, masthead, and business plan. Allow me to explain why.

Research is a foundational component that *precedes* the actual development, manufacturing, or launch of any product, initiative, or idea. Research and Development departments focus on different things, and to a large extent, bring different value to a problem and its solution.

Think of researchers as scouts. They're the people who are out in the dark, fishing around for a pair of night vision goggles, trying to assess whether they're on the right mountain, running random tests, and looking for higher ground. Their investigations are ongoing and open-ended.

Developers, on the other hand, are climbers. They're the people running up the mountain as fast as they can to the top (working in "sprints"), building products, touching the nuts and bolts along the way, and working toward a hard deliverable.

On an individual level, while we are naturally inclined to one functionality over the other, we all have a little bit of researcher/scout and a little bit of developer/climber within us, and we must know how to perform both functions. Otherwise, we will never climb the tallest mountain; we will continue to climb the wrong one.

Don't Wait for Necessity to Be the Mother of Invention

Nintendo has been in the gaming business since Fusajiro Yamauchi founded it in 1889. Yamauchi was a craftsman who made traditional Japanese playing cards called hanafuda, which were initially distributed to Russian prisoners during the Russo-Japanese War and were later exported internationally. Nintendo remained in the playing card business until it branched out to board games in the 1960s.

By the time early computing and arcade video games took hold in the late 1970s, Fusajiro's son, Hiroshi, was running the company, and its very survival was suddenly in dire jeopardy. Hiroshi was scrambling in development mode, trying to stay relevant in a rapidly changing market and outrun international competition by iterating on their existing product line, making cheaper versions of the playing cards and board games with slightly different images. It wasn't working. The company was doing worse and worse, and the situation became desperate.

Hiroshi realized the family business was about to go bankrupt. He was forced, out of necessity, to stop and think, "Playing cards is a losing battle, how do I get out of this?" For the first time in many generations, he looked at the problem differently.

With this new outlook, and the urgency associated with it, he switched from development mode into research mode. Hiroshi recognized he had an audience for fictional characters, and he could test new ideas on them to try an X. He decided to drop the physical element of his playing cards altogether and focus on digital characters instead. Rather than climb the physical card or board game mountain, he started up the digital gaming mountain.

Hiroshi's efforts didn't pay off immediately. The gaming market crash of 1983 wiped out the vast majority of the North American market, including the lynchpin, Atari. While other companies were tanking left and right, Nintendo used its key asset – fictional characters – and tested variations of them on its existing audience. It launched Donkey Kong in 1981, Super Mario Bros. in 1985, Game Boy and Tetris in 1989, and the Nintendo home entertainment system in 1991. Under Hiroshi's leadership, Nintendo became the biggest company in the video gaming industry. His father and grandfather saw their business as playing cards, but Hiroshi realized it was actually the business of fictional characters.

Like Fosbury, Hiroshi knew he couldn't succeed with incremental improvements. If the company was not at risk of immanent failure, he may never have moved into digital at all. (He wouldn't have needed to!) As with Fosbury, necessity was the mother of his invention. Hiroshi asked himself, "What can I do to get out of this losing business and onto a completely different playing field?"

Too often, we hear about people or companies that came up with some type of innovative solution or product as a result of having their backs up against the wall. Only due to extreme necessity did they pivot out of the slightly better iterative A/B mode into a deeper, exploratory, research X mode. And what about the rest of us who don't find our backs against the wall, and probably never even looked for X?

We don't need to wait for necessity to be the mother of invention. Most of us go through life taking small and calculated steps toward the top of the mountains we're climbing without looking up to see whether we're climbing the right mountain. We are content to do just a little bit better at what we're doing without questioning if the direction itself is still a good one. And what a shame that is because we are settling for the incremental gains. Every so often, we need to stop what we're doing (steady A/B testing) and take a giant leap to test whether our ongoing efforts are in the right direction (test X). If we don't, we're heading toward a Local Maximum, which is not a terrible outcome, but it's no Dick Fosbury, Dan Wieden, or Nintendo.

A Little Byte of Data Science

The problem of A/B testing is a huge one for computers, and it costs companies billions of dollars in lost revenue. If you figure Amazon pays its delivery drivers $20 per hour, the drivers make 10 to 15 deliveries per hour, and the company makes 3.5 million deliveries a day, you can understand why calculating the best delivery route is worth a fortune.

So, how does Amazon Prime overcome its A/B routing challenge? It builds X into its method. As a climber asks,

"What direction should I head?" Amazon's delivery algorithm starts by asking the big questions: What does the best route look like? and What is the optimal starting point? As mentioned, the algorithm can't check every possibility (there are far too many), but after a few queries, it will pick a general direction. In other words, it chooses which mountain to climb. After which, it starts making increasingly smaller optimizations to the route (it begins to climb the mountain).

As with other A/B testing methods, the approach leads to a maximum, but typically a local one. Amazon, therefore, forces the algorithm to add an X every few A/B iterations, which could be classified as starting the route from a different point or changing many of the route points in one go. If the X result is terrible, it will continue with A/B testing (until it tries for another X). But if the X result is good, it will improve on it, rather than continue with the A/B testing.

Google Search works in a similar fashion when choosing the 10 best results to a query. During the fraction of a second a user waits to see the results, Google runs A/B tests, switching different results in and out to see what combination scores best. Like Amazon, Google doesn't run A/B tests exclusively. It adds an X every few tests to continually ensure it's not missing a better mountain somewhere. And naturally, it sends its Xs (or shall I say, scouts) in directions it identifies as potentially interesting to learn more about its surroundings.

To reduce the risk of reaching a Local Maximum, data scientists are regularly forcing their algorithms to periodically check for X, which is similar to lifting their heads up to ensure they are climbing the right mountain.

Chapter 3

Training to Overcome the Valley of Death

Your attitude, not your aptitude, will determine your altitude.

– Zig Ziglar

Avraham, an Ethiopian Israeli, is caught in a trap that will affect the rest of his life. When he was 18, he joined the military like every other Israeli citizen. He excelled during his three years of mandatory service and, for the first time in his life, was given a promotion and responsibility for a small group of soldiers whom he commanded. Even though the pay was less than minimum wage, the military provided food and clothing and very little time or opportunity to spend whatever earnings he received. By the end of his service, the 21-year-old Avraham has no job or degree, just the $15,000 he saved over three years.

Avraham knows he's behind on his career path, and he knows he needs to catch up, especially if he is to be married by 25 as is expected in the Ethiopian community. But he's burned out from military service, and he has a strong inclination to use his $15,000 of his savings and travel to Thailand for six months. Thousands of others in Avraham's situation have the same desire.

33

A year later, now 22, Avraham needs to take the GMAT and redo a few high-school exams before he can start university. His bank account is running low. Soldiers from economically stable backgrounds would typically enroll in university at this point. Those who served in elite units, especially those who accumulated unique technological know-how, are often offered lucrative jobs with leading hi-tech companies or go on to create start-ups. But for those from poorer backgrounds, who have not accumulated skill sets that translate into paying jobs, military service tends to prevent them from pursuing a degree or developing a marketable skill. The lucky ones may get a minimum wage paying job. But very few can afford to work a low-wage, part-time job *and* pursue a three-year degree to learn the skills needed to secure a higher paying job in the future.

Avraham finds himself standing at the edge of just such a Local Maximum. He is typical of thousands of Israeli soldiers who have also reached a Local Maximum at the completion of their military service. He dedicated three years to his country, and although he developed strong character traits and a knack for basic managerial tasks, he finds himself without a degree, any tradable skills, or capital he can fall back on at the age of 22.

Looking at the statistics, the Israeli government realized many young people like Avraham, and especially those from poor and/or immigrant backgrounds, were forced into less-than-ideal situations. In response, they designed a plan with the intention of offering a path over the valley, away from the Local Maximum.

At the heart of the program, the government created a list of jobs, specifically ones with labor shortages the government was keen to fill. They allowed post-army soldiers to work in those jobs, tax-free, and at a slightly higher hourly wage than they would normally pay. For example, gas station attendants are usually in short supply. So, let's say the average pay for gas station attendants is $10.50 an hour. The government offers people in its program $12.50 an hour, tax-free, instead. The combination of a tax-free, higher hourly wage is significant. The intent of the program was to solve two problems at once: fill a labor shortage and assist post-army individuals to make enough money to work through university.

Let's explore how this government-backed program works for Avraham. He is still keen to travel to Thailand and unwind after his service. The government will not penalize him for this decision; many leading psychologists suggest an extended vacation after service is highly beneficial. Economists tend to agree and have noted that well-traveled individuals contribute to Israel's overall multicultural and globally minded diversity. So, without fear of losing his government nest egg, Avraham departs for Thailand for five months (instead of six, as he has less money to spend) with enthusiasm.

Crucially, when Avraham returns from his much-needed rest and exploration, he can turn to the list of tax-free, government-identified jobs reserved for people like him. He feels optimistic because he's been able to travel, he can pursue a degree, there is a job waiting for him, and he can cover his immediate costs.

Sounds like a win-win, right?

Teach a Man to Code

My friend Takala, the CEO of the incredible Israeli NGO Tech-Career Israel,[1] emphatically says, "Wrong!" Like Avraham, Takala is an Ethiopian Israeli. He arrived in Israel at the age of 14 and knows firsthand how difficult it is to integrate into Israeli society as an Ethiopian immigrant. Most of the people in his community immigrated to Israel as young children. Over the years, they learned to speak Hebrew. Many of them achieved a high school diploma. They have spent years and effort assimilating into modern Israeli lifestyle, but arriving at adulthood, the reality of their situation was still apparent: their parents arrived in the country with little means and no access to a strategic network of people to help give them and their kids a leg up. Most Ethiopian Israelis in the original immigrant generation have struggled to adjust and establish themselves professionally to the level of their Israeli-born peers.

As a former Israeli soldier himself, Takala immediately recognized the Local Maximum his community and people like Avraham faced, as well as the inadequacies of the government initiatives to help. When Avraham came back from traveling in Thailand, he secured one of the government job listings with the intention of enrolling at a local university. The $12.50 hourly, untaxed wage seemed like a lot of money, especially compared to what he made in the military. After a few months of working full-time, he lost the immediate drive to get a higher degree and rationalized that he still had time. At 25, as planned, he married, and his expenses soared. He needed to provide for his wife's family in addition to his own, and soon, he was barely scraping by financially. Three, four, then five years passed, and Avraham never did enroll for a degree. He also never acquired training for new skills that would lift him into a higher pay bracket. He received a few raises here and there, but never enough to make a significant difference or allow him to change his circumstances. To cross from the mountain he was on, over to a higher, better one, he had to overcome a daunting valley that seemed to grow vaster with each passing year.

Takala says, "We, at Tech-Career, want more for the Ethiopian community. The government incentives are great but we, as a community, are not identical. For a large portion of us, having access to a program that helps us get a job, especially a safe job, is great. Don't get me wrong. I am a teacher, and our staff is primarily made up of educators. Our relatives and spouses are nurses and policemen. I think these are the greatest and most fulfilling roles, and teaching is what I love most. But these jobs don't pay very much, and crucially, even if you're the best at your job, your paycheck doesn't increase much over the years. If you're very lucky, you may just outpace inflation over the course of your career. As a community, we need high-paying jobs as well."

To his immense credit, Takala identified the Local Maximum and specifically the deep valley his community was confronted with. He knew there had to be a way to build a bridge across that valley so Ethiopian Israelis had access to the same mountains as the rest of Israel's citizens.

In 2002, Takala embarked on a mountain climbing journey of his own. He wanted to create an organization that could assist his underserved and underemployed community. He began with a few simple questions: What jobs are in short supply, have salaries that scale, and ideally, scale fast? His conclusion: teach Ethiopians to code. He was not wrong. Even in the lower, entry-level, quality assurance (QA) coding positions, salaries are 30% to 40% higher than a teacher's. Most crucially, a QA developer with five years of experience could make double their initial salary. Double! Over the course of a career, someone with the right training and job placement assistance could make five to six times the salary of a teacher. Consider the impact this kind of training could have on someone like Avraham.

Takala knew the biggest challenge for Ethiopian Israelis was not brainpower, aptitude, drive, or ability. It was that they did not have access to opportunities to learn the skills necessary to compete for high-income jobs. From this insight and inspiration, Tech-Career was born as a bridge to overcome the valley and put Ethiopian Israelis on the right mountains.

Almost half of Tech-Career's incoming students live below the poverty level and work in low-wage, low-skilled jobs. Run by Ethiopians for Ethiopians, the aim is to convert gas station workers into engineers. "This means we will have many more Ethiopian homeowners, maybe even some millionaires who will break into other parts of society and challenge the stigma the community faces," Takala says of his company's mission.

He is careful to explain the challenges involved. "This is not for everyone. We have a rigorous process on our end to make sure the system works. Ahead of each new academic year, we review our strategy and match what the market needs with what we can achieve with our pupils in 10 months. We don't have a long training period because we cover our students' costs and accommodations, and we need to finish before the next year's batch of students comes in. Plus, there is a lot to cover. Our typical student doesn't know how to speak English. We need to teach them the coding language and the spoken language so that they can interview with tech companies. Some of our students have a poor background in math as well. We accept one out of every four applicants. They must have a high school diploma and have completed their full military service. We test their IQ in a variety of ways, but mainly we are looking for the people who are willing to work hard. The 10-month program is 6 days a week and requires roughly 12 hours a day of studying."

Further, he says, "Last year we accepted 130 out of 450 applicants and taught four classes: two QA, one Python, and one JAVA. We optimize for which students are likely to do best in each class. I am happy to boast that 92% of our students have made it into high-tech positions. The majority of them are already making more money than we are here at Tech-Career in just their first year."

When I asked Takala the secret of his 92% success rate, he said, "We have to make sure we are aiming at the right fields, getting the right teachers, and building a strong network of hiring companies. But that is all secondary. Coding is unique as you are tested entirely by what you can do, not by what certificates or diplomas you have. Our students understand this, and they understand they have 10 very challenging months to get through. But they also understand those 10 months can lead them to an entirely different career path, so they work their butts off."

He highlights two core focuses. "First, we need to make the process of becoming an engineer as short as possible with as high a success rate as possible. Second, we must keep ensuring that the skills they are acquiring here are best suited to the economy, so our graduates do really well in their jobs."

"For the applicant," he explains, "the central concern is around the length of the program. Typically, the graduates, who are a year or two into their new careers, truly appreciate how much this new career path leads them to a better life. Now, we regularly bring graduates in to share their experiences, and especially contrast their current situation with their old gas station jobs."

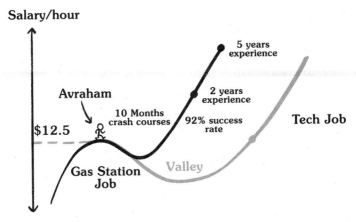

Avraham is currently stuck at a Local Maximum. He is earning $12.50 an hour – better than any other job he could currently get. To move over to the tech industry, he would have to study for four years, without earning much in parallel, only to apply for a job that he will hopefully get. This presents a large and painful valley. Tech-Career offers a short path, with high success probability, to the "Tech Job Mountain," which Avraham can then climb.

Having worked with Tech-Career as a volunteer for many years, I've seen its remarkable success in moving their community members off a high point on a low mountain to a low point on a high mountain. They are effectively helping people cross the valley and break employment barriers by providing training and opportunities for socioeconomic mobility.

The challenge of "crossing valleys" is not unique to Ethiopian Israeli soldiers, but this case highlights one of the most common and painful Local Maximum tragedies, which is being able to see a better mountain but not being able to get there. Takala's principles are clear: shorten the valley, while highlighting how much greener the grass really is on the other side.

Shorten the Valley of Death

When implementing the first principle, it is important to differentiate between narrowing the valley versus reducing its depth. Narrowing a valley means you will reach the other mountain quicker, while reducing its depth means there is less of a descent. Knowing when to use each can make all the difference.

For example, consider the challenge faced by many of the poor farmers in Africa. They don't produce enough to put aside some food as a back-up for a rainy day. Nor do they have enough surplus to sell some and buy better equipment for the next season, so that they can produce more. The width of the valley is not the biggest problem; it's the depth of the valley. Taking a step down from where they are by saving seeds or selling part of their food would lead to starvation.

Think of it this way: If you ask a wealthy investor for one million dollars and guarantee to give him two million dollars back, his first question (if he believes your guarantee) is how long before he sees the return. He doesn't have a problem giving you a million dollars (to take a step down from your mountain), but the length of time the endeavor will take is the challenge.

We often face wide or deep valleys in our personal and professional lives, and sometimes we even exchange one type for the other. For example, few of us have enough money to purchase a house outright with cash. Even if we were promised a $2,000 cash infusion every month for twenty years, it wouldn't change the fact that we can't buy the house today. This is a deep valley. However, securing a mortgage transforms the deep valley to a shallower one that we can slowly and steadily overcome, through smaller monthly payments versus paying for the entire cost of the home upfront.

At Tech-Career, Takala realized the valley of a traditional university degree was too wide for many of the people in his community to traverse. "Our students are very bright, and they are capable of doing really well on any single test," Takala explains. "It is just that a three- or even four-year degree is not an option for most of them because of the financial pressure." Takala made the valley less wide by shortening the length of his training program to 10 months so students can enter the job market faster, and less deep by covering their costs for this period of time.

How Much Greener Is the Other Side?

This second principle for overcoming the valley may be intuitive, but not many follow it. We assume, "All I need to know is that the other mountain is higher." However, discovering exactly how much better the other mountain is than the one you are on can dramatically affect the way you act.

Successful start-up founders use this insight regularly when pitching to investors. Likely, their achievements to date are not as impressive as what they envision down the road. So, they focus on painting a vivid picture of what they expect to achieve in the future. These founders realize that educating their audience about the future of their venture is more enticing than talking about the mountain they're on currently, and it can make the difference between investors choosing to jump aboard or stay out. Clarifying exactly how much greener the other side is can dramatically affect tangible actions, and it determines whether it's worth the journey to get there.

For example, think about the original idea for developing an electric hybrid car. The average car drives 25 MPG (miles per gallon). Imagine if the manufacturers pitched a hybrid with an entirely different motor, battery, and all new power electronics that will get drivers to 27 MPG. No one is going to bite on such a slim marginal improvement. The grass is only slightly greener, and the valley is too costly. But, when the hybrid manufacturers pitch investors on the same dynamics at a 50-MPG capability, we're looking at a significantly greener pasture. The effort to cross this valley is appealing, and investors will gladly strap on their hiking boots to begin the descent.

Alternatively, consider pitching a newly developed antifraud software to banks. This new software will increase transaction security from 99% to 99.9%. The entrepreneurs are not going to say, "Hey, buy my software, you'll see less than a 1% increase." No. That's not appealing. They're going to say, "My software guarantees 90% less fraud." Though the math works out to be the same, they're going to paint a greener picture of the future to secure interest and investment.

One of the companies we at Hetz Ventures first backed, Trigo,[2] were able to demonstrate how much greener their technology made the other side look. Trigo had a vision to deliver autonomous shopping into grocery stores, meaning people can walk into a store, collect what they want to buy, and walk out without having to queue up in a line or interact with a salesperson. They had some of the best engineers on the planet working to build this vision and were able to secure $200 million for the idea even before it was fully developed. Trigo's product doesn't promise incremental improvements of 5% to 10% increased efficiency. It's closer to 100%, and that's a valley investors can see across.

Takala does this with applicants to Tech-Career's program. But for him, it's not just about finding some fancy way to play with the numbers. He offers something deeply meaningful and life changing, and he wants applicants to see how much greener the other side of the valley is. This is why he regularly brings graduates of the program in to describe how much better their lives are now than they would have been if they'd stayed on their previous mountains.

Even graduates who are only one or two years out of the program, who are not yet pulling in huge salaries, are able to get a significant leg up by doing things they weren't able to do before, such as securing a mortgage. And it's not because banks are warm, loving entities. It's because banks know they can underwrite mortgages for entry-level engineers on a stable career trajectory more securely than they can for gas station attendants, who are not. The greenery on the other side offers value beyond monetary security. It also translates to lifestyle changes, such as access to advanced training, mental health services, more fulfilling work, and a higher, smarter caliber of colleagues. For anyone debating a career change, learning about how much happier you have the potential to be is likely to affect your decision, no less so than changing the valley length or depth you have to overcome.

Takala and Tech-Career work tirelessly to help their Ethiopian students understand and overcome the valley they face. However, there is one element they ignore. Not out of ignorance, but because they can afford to. When standing at a Local Maximum, the first step you have to take is down. You have to make the decision to get off the mountain you're standing on. Each of the 130 students Tech-Career accepts per session (out of 450 applicants) have already committed to taking that first step down simply by applying to the program. They've already done the mental work to realize the effort of going down their current mountain and crossing the valley is worth it.

Building Bridges

Overcoming the valley, as mentioned, is a common challenge for early-stage start-ups. The two young founders of Granulate[3] faced this obstacle when they were pitching a new technology to optimize the load-balancing feature utilized by a wide range of companies to enhance the performance and reliability of their websites.

Every time a computer receives an instruction, or a task, it must decide which server to send the task to. So, if I'm Netflix and I have thousands of machines running my operation, and Jimmy wants to watch *Game of Thrones* and Joanna wants to watch *Hunger Games*, my internal system has to decide which machine to send the requests to, and quickly. The load balancer is the device that makes these types of decisions.

The Granulate founders were longtime friends who served together in the military. They are unassuming, quiet fellows, but extremely confident in their technology, and with good reason. They built a solution that could dramatically improve the tradeoff large corporations often need to make between running things faster and running things at a lower cost. Granulate solved for both in parallel.

Hetz was among Granulate's earliest investors, and, lo and behold, when we tested their technology internally, it was – as promised – dramatically better than anyone else's. Staggeringly better, in fact, and it showed huge gains in both efficiency and speed. We took the technology to some of the largest companies in the world to demo, and said, "Listen, you can implement this cutting-edge development at no cost. It's going to save you a ton of money." But even though the technology worked perfectly, and everyone was impressed by its speed and efficiency, no one bought it.

Why? Because the executives at these huge corporations took one look at these two unknown, unassuming, shy Israelis with a tiny, unheard-of company and said, "There's no freaking way we're going to put our entire multi-billion-dollar system onto your load balancer. It's suicide. We'd much rather bank on a less sophisticated balancer that has been tested a gazillion times and costs us millions of dollars every single day than bank on these guys."

There was no debate that Granulate represented a much higher and greener mountain than the one they were on. The problem was the valley was too scary; they couldn't justify the risk. They weren't prepared to rely entirely on a small start-up they'd never heard of before.

After much internal debate about how to handle the strange predicament of sitting on a potential goldmine of a solution, with nothing but upside, and a fat stack of "nos" from the biggest companies in the world, Granulate decided to pivot. They made it less painful for the target companies to step down from the mountain they were on by building a bridge across the valley. And the way they did this was instead of selling the technology as a load balancer, they sold it as a virtual agent, meaning they built a fail-safe protection into the technology. If the load balancing function started to fail, instead of the whole system crashing, the function would revert back to the company's original (and antiquated) load balancer. At any given point in time, if things didn't work out over on the higher, greener mountain, the company could slide back to the peak they were currently on.

Within 24 months, Granulate went from near bankruptcy to a $650 million acquisition by Intel. The tough times tend to bring people closer, much more so than the easy times. When Asaf Ezra, the CEO, asked me to make the best man speech at his wedding a few months after the acquisition, I was pleased to be able to tell him that his marriage was the only bridge I had seen him build where no fallback was required.

The Judo Push

In 2010, a series of uprisings swept across the Middle East and North Africa, marking a turning point in the region's history. Sparked by the frustrations of ordinary citizens in the region, who yearned for political freedom, economic opportunity, and an end to corruption and authoritarian rule, the Arab Spring was an organic movement that caught many intelligence agencies off guard. The initial protests in Tunisia quickly spread to Egypt, Libya, Yemen, and Syria, among others. Intelligence agencies found themselves ill-prepared to accurately assess the magnitude and consequences of the uprisings, highlighting their limited understanding of the deep-rooted societal grievances that fueled the popular discontent.

In our highly classified Israeli Intelligence unit, we watched these developments from our desks and scratched our heads. As an intelligence service, a critical underlying assumption has always been that we can understand a region by staying on top of the key people. For instance, if we knew what Hosni Mubarak, the Egyptian president, and his close circle were thinking, we could assume we'd have a good understanding of how Egypt would behave in different scenarios. But at that point in time, even the Egyptian president didn't know what was going to happen. If you drew a grid connecting Egypt, Syria, Jordan, Tunisia, Iraq, Libya, and other states that quickly found themselves in the midst of an existential uprising, you'd find Israel geographically in the middle.

For my colleagues and me in the intelligence community, the events surrounding Arab Spring put us in a tough position. We needed a fast solution to cope with the unrest. But for a unit that planned major classified intelligence operations, our operation cycle from planning stage to execution was typically four to five years. How could we justify immediately investing major resources in the short term when it was so unclear who our target would be in more than a few years' time?

As an officer, my team and I were charged with an unusual mission. Rather than improve our intelligence capabilities within a specific domain, we needed to dramatically decrease the time needed to execute complex operations. "In a world where uncertainty is so vast," the generals told me, "it is critical we shorten our cycle from five years to two, and ultimately to 10 months." That was a big valley to overcome, and with uncertainty on the target subject (or shall I say, mountain), it was hard to justify. The generals were speaking, literally, in Local Maximum terminology.

During this process, there were major technological and operational challenges, as to be expected, but the critical obstacle we did not foresee was a mental one. As we moved through the development stages, we reached the critical point where we needed a major investment. It required resources be diverted from other operations, and this became a sticking point even though the generals had instructed me to shorten the valley.

Every week, I presented the generals with an update and, although it was apparent that pursuing our operation was necessary and wise (especially as the level of uncertainty continued to increase), they struggled to justify the required expenditure. All of the other officers, who went into the room before me to present their updates (pitch for resources), were focused on other missions with clear targets, but I couldn't even give a sense of who my target was. How could the generals justify diverting resources away from clear targets to one that was unknown? The other officers were pitching mountain peaks, and I was pitching a shorter valley.

As time went on without funding, my team realized the psychological challenge inherent to our particular valley could jeopardize our entire operation. We needed cyber units, tech systems, engineers, and other classified capabilities, but we couldn't paint a picture powerful enough to convince the generals to give up the mountain peaks in exchange for shortening the valley. We couldn't persuade them to take that first step down, off our Local Maximum.

Many scientific experiments prove that people prefer to stick with what they have, even when the logical decision is to try something different (Status Quo Bias). This is especially true when a lot of effort has already been invested (Sunk Cost Bias). In my case, the Status Quo Bias had a strong hold, and because the military had been working in a particular way for many years, the Sunk Cost Bias was extra high too. Three months went by.

Our breakthrough came in a surprising manner. One of my soldiers, a former international Judo champion, was reminiscing about the painful preparation he underwent to fit into a lighter weight bracket. He recalled having to literally starve himself before the official weigh-ins and even monitor the milliliters of water he could drink. "If a coach wanted to push us to lose more weight, he would make us train in the higher weight bracket for a session or two. The difference between the two brackets is enormous. I couldn't even make it through the first round in the heavier weight class, never mind win a competition. Feeling the pain, and the physical punches from those much heavier guys, gave me the push I needed to get into the weight bracket I could be competitive in." Unofficially around the judo, the coach's technique of demonstrating the pain of the current suboptimal strategy was known as the "Judo Push".

At the next weekly update with the generals, we decided rather than trying to sell them on the dangers of our unidentifiable target, we would try a "Judo Push" instead. We wanted to give the generals a sense of how much we are missing by staying in the Status Quo. I remember the look on their faces when they saw our first slide titled: "Our latest big intelligence misses." The rest of the slides elaborately described every major opportunity we had lost over the previous 6 months as a result of not being funded to conduct operations within a 10-month frame. We highlighted both the objective of each opportunity and the value lost. A few weeks later, we finally had our resources.

I can't say I blame the generals for taking so long to come around. People tend to focus on the mountain peaks – and those who reach the top get the credit – even though we know that how we traverse the landscape and manage the valleys is what makes the real difference. And sometimes, we need a Judo Push to get us off our current Maximum.

In 2013, my unit's new approach to shortening the valley was nominated for the IDF's leading creativity award. We didn't win that year, as the approach "hadn't [yet] produced a clear intelligence achievement," or in Local Maximum terminology, they hadn't yet reached the peak. But by 2014, we successfully overcame the valley *and* climbed the better mountain; and we won the top prize.

Learning to overcome valleys to reach a taller mountain is critical for navigating ourselves away from Local Maximums. To do so, we must first look for ways to shorten the valley, either its length or its depth. Then, we gather as much information about the mountain we are trying to reach, as some of these learnings can affect our decisions on our current mountain. And finally, we find the confidence to take that first step down, which very well might be the best decision we ever make.

A Little Byte of Data Science

A key concern software engineers face is that their algorithms will give up before they find the higher mountain. They worry the algorithm won't get through the valley and will revert back to an original Local Maximum because the valley is too vast to cross. This is especially true in situations where the field is both enormous and highly unpredictable. Recall our Granulate example. The early buyers were too afraid to cross the vast valley and walked away from a significantly higher mountain, which was the revolutionary load balancing technology.

Another example of trying to navigate this type of terrain can be found in healthcare, and specifically in trying to predict protein folding, or how proteins will stick together. If you've ever wondered why we haven't found a cure for cancer or chronic pain, one reason is because algorithms face their own "Valleys of Death," whereby they have to keep moving in a direction that isn't scoring them a higher value, and possibly scores them an even lower value. The cost of such a predicament is enormous, because, often times, they're not just missing out on a few percentage points or incremental gains; they're missing out on an entirely new set of opportunities. The engineers know this, and in the data science world, these valleys are a real nightmare to deal with.

Biologically, our bodies contain over 10,000 types of protein, each made through a physical process where a protein chain folds to make a 3D structure with specific characteristics. Predicting how each protein will fold together, however, is nearly impossible. Machines can only calculate a small fraction of the options (similar to the Amazon Prime delivery route and Google Search examples). Scientists test the options they anticipate are the most relevant, and a key method they use is to provide their algorithms with a high degree of momentum, which ensures directional consistency. So, if the algorithm finds something of relevance in a certain direction, it won't stop and reverse immediately. (Think of the Road Runner in the Bugs Bunny cartoons, racing at top speed. Even when he's headed over the side of a cliff, his feet continue to move.) Data scientists trade off faster adjustments to keep moving and reduce the risk of getting stuck at a Local Maximum.

(continued)

(continued)

Takala integrates momentum at Tech-Career by having his graduates sign two- or three-year contracts with their new hi-tech employers. Often, their salaries are staggered in advance, meaning, they are told what their raises will be at the end of the first and second years. Like the Road Runner, Takala wants to make it more difficult for his graduates to stop before the many career benefits will kick in.

Chapter 4

Agility to Navigate the Unexpected

It is not the strongest of the species that survive, nor the most intelligent, but the one most responsive to change.

— Charles Darwin

It was the year 2000, when Netflix CEO Marc Randolph and co-founder Reed Hastings chartered a private plane from California to Dallas, Texas, to meet with Blockbuster's CEO, John Antioco. It took months to arrange a meeting, but it was finally confirmed at the last minute. Famously, the Netflix co-founders flew in after an alcohol-fueled company retreat, wearing shorts and flipflops,[1] to present a merger proposal for Blockbuster to acquire their fledgling start-up. The asking price was $50 million.[2] As we all know, the deal never materialized.

In his book, *That Will Never Work: The Birth of Netflix and the Amazing Life of an Idea*,[3] Randolph recalls the disastrous meeting, where Antioco essentially had to choke back his laughter in the face of the proposal. Acquiring Netflix made zero sense to Blockbuster. Following a merger deal with Viacom, the company was worth $8.4 billion and had been crowned the undisputed "King of the Video Rental Industry."

51

But the laughter quickly died down. Although there was nothing Blockbuster couldn't replicate in Netflix's model (and they likely ended up spending 10 times more on advertising, content, user interface, and other costs), Netflix is now a now a noun and a verb worth over $271 billion,[4] and Blockbuster went bust. Remarkably, even in 2008, only two years before filing for bankruptcy, Blockbuster's Antioco said, "I've been frankly confused by this fascination that everybody has with Netflix. . .Netflix doesn't really have or do anything that we can't or don't already do ourselves."[5]

The Blockbuster vs. Netflix tale is an eye-opening example of the powerful effect of a Local Maximum. Blockbuster had everything going for it: a global reach of contracts with the leading content producers plus a 28-day exclusivity over any competitor, a huge network of stores across all 50 states, deep pockets of capital, and a strong brand. Importantly, as Blockbuster executives said multiple times throughout their sparring history, there was nothing Netflix did or invented that Blockbuster could not replicate easily. There was no impregnable IP, technology, or secret Coca-Cola ingredient.

If you Google "why Blockbuster failed," you are likely to get a blend of tactical errors such as the company's obsession with late fees (which accounted for more than 15% of its revenue), poor customer service, and inattention to customer preferences. If you read one of the Ivy League case studies on the topic you will hear of the strategic errors, executional mistakes, and closed-minded senior management. The company's documented errors certainly contributed to Blockbuster's historic failure, but what if there is something deeper? What if it was already clear by 2000 that Netflix would be the obvious winner, Blockbuster was near its peak, and its senior management had to get everything right to survive rather than just not go wrong?

When They Go Deep, We Go Wide

One day in July, our entire elite combat unit was at the beach for our annual "Special Unit Day": a day of "relaxation" military style (meaning we were given eight minutes rather than seven to pitch all the tents and indulge in similar forms of relaxing). As the youngest squadron, we arrived earlier than everyone else to do the preparation work. While unpacking the Jeeps, our officer signaled us over, and in a deadly serious voice said, "Every year, there is a digging competition. Two soldiers are chosen from each squadron and compete to see who can dig the deepest hole. We MUST win this. There is no other possible outcome."

Yes, it was *that* kind of "relaxation." Actually, this was not a joke for our officer; he was determined to prove to the unit's senior commanders he meant business. (Yes, through a hole digging competition at the beach.) We found out later the youngest squadron had never won the hole digging competition, but our officer was having none of that. He decided to run a pre-competition try-out before the rest of the unit arrived to determine which one of us should represent the squadron in this critical moment. Under our officer's command, we stopped the preparations for the fun beach day and paired up. At the last minute, our officer decided to join the competition, too, and paired himself up with me.

All ten pairs, including the officer and myself, knelt in the sand and awaited his instructions: "Guys, this is a seven-minute dig; deepest hole wins. Ready, set, dig!"

Within seconds, the whole group transformed into sand-digging maniacs. Sand was flying everywhere, including all over each other. Grown men were yelling instructions to their digging partners. It was mad. And soon enough, though it felt like an hour, the seven minutes were finally over. Frankly, most of us didn't care about the competition and definitely didn't want to be the representative in this odd contest, but we worried about underperforming in front of the officer. A respectable third place seemed the ideal outcome to most of us.

We stood silently in pairs beside our sand holes; sweat pouring down our backs. The officer took a long stick and measured each hole as he walked by, cutting a line in the wood to mark the depth. At the end, he re-measured the three deepest holes, one of which was the one he and I dug, and announced a tie between ours and another team's. Our officer decided to send the other pair to the competition to represent us, and we all gave the winning pair a warm round of applause.

When our officer wandered off, we examined the different holes. At first, it was very obvious that the winners' hole was clearly the deepest, as the one our officer and I dug was a good few inches shallower. But then I noticed another clear pattern: the winning hole had an ideal shape. It wasn't a skinny narrow one, but rather a wider one that made it easier for two pairs of hands to remove lots of sand in parallel. And then, at the very bottom, the shape changed into a skinny hole. The skinny narrow holes were good at first but gradually the narrowness limited the digging pair's ability to keep up the pace. Only one hand could fit down into the sand hole at a time, and eventually, all the narrow holes stopped at roughly the length of an arm.

With my new finding, I mustered up the courage to share this piece of sensitive information with our officer. Soon enough, we were ordered to scrap the beach day preparation work (again) and focus on testing out sand-hole-digging strategies to determine the best shape. The optimal result, we discovered, came from two minutes of digging an extra-wide hole, which the diggers could kneel into, four minutes of digging a medium-wide hole below the widest section, and a final one-minute sprint to dig the narrowest bit at the bottom. It's fair to say, when the rest of the units arrived at the beach, they were slightly taken back with how little we had managed to set up.

The actual beach day was nice, if not slightly awkward. As the youngest squadron, we were told to stay in uniform while the senior guys bathed in swimwear, but we knew our moment to shine was coming. As the sun started to set, the head of unit signaled it was time to kick off the official sand-digging competition. As each officer chose two soldiers from his squadron to compete, our officer pretended to randomly choose the winning pair from our earlier trial-run contest.

Ready, Set, Go! The race was on; again there was sand flying everywhere and much screaming between the pairs at work while everyone else cheered them on. Our representatives were the weakest physically. In only 12 months of training, they had not yet undergone the muscle building process the older squadrons had, but our guys had a clear plan. Watching the competition felt like flipping through TV channels: one moment, everyone was relaxing at the beach, and the next, there was a ferocious sandstorm accompanied by howling soldiers, and finally, complete silence. The seven minutes were up, and the unit commander marched along to examine the sand holes and measure the results with his stick.

To everyone's astonishment, the commander announced it was too close to call, and he added three minutes of extra time. Within seconds, sand was flying again. This time, though, it was clear the shape of the sand holes made a big difference. Most of the teams employed the same strategy we had used earlier in the day: two people furiously digging until only one pair of hands could fit within the narrowing width of the hole. The final digger was lying on his belly, digging until the length of his arm could dig no deeper. Eventually, most of the pairs had one member sitting idle while the other member (with the longest arms), kept going. Only, our representatives had all four hands digging. They spent the first minute widening their base again to get lower and then dig down further.

This time there was no question: we won. Yes, the scrappy junior soldiers in full uniform pulled off an unlikely victory. Everyone else pretended like they didn't care, and resumed swimming and laughing in the water, but our officer was right. Winning the sand digging competition sent a strong message: the new guys are tough.

Were we? Almost certainly not. But we tempered muscle with agility and won the game as a result.

Balancing Muscle and Agility

Until now, we have analyzed the Local Maximum challenges from a fairly level playing field. The assumption has been that we all have the same capabilities to climb a mountain and the same agility to adapt from one mountain to another, but the reality is different. Our strategies, culture, and other elements shape us and our organizations to the degree that some are more agile while others are better at muscling through.

For example, the CEO of a publicly owned company can't adapt as easily to market shifts as a privately owned company CEO.

The former must make sure he hits his quarterly milestones. He must provide highly scrutinized public reporting that affects his share price. For a private CEO, on the other hand, it can be enough to have a few conversations with his key investors in advance of making a big change. The public CEO might find it easier to raise capital, as he is liquid, whereas a private company might struggle. Or an accounting student who does his minor in transfer pricing is more likely to get a high-earning specialized job, but he might find it harder to make a career change than an accounting student who did his minor in marketing.

We often trade off muscle and agility, not just when we decide how to spend a 60-minute workout, but also when we think about how to build our careers and organizations. We focus on moats, barriers to entry, expertise, or as *Harvard Business Review* refers to our time, "the age of hyper-specializing."[6] And this focus may help us build muscle or enhance productivity; it also increases our likelihood of reaching a Local Maximum. Imagine a competitive bodybuilder learning that his upcoming competition will require some element of flexibility instead of just lifting weights. He has built up muscle but isn't agile enough to adapt to a change.

Let's take another look at Blockbuster vs. Netflix. Blockbuster had everything Netflix had; it actually had even more. It had 9,000 physical stores and 65 million registered customers. It had 84,000 employees and was owed millions of dollars in late payment fees. Did these assets equate to a true advantage? As long as the target didn't change, and the goal was to become the largest DVD rental company, yes. They helped the company climb the DVD mountain and provided a muscle moat to defend its business as well. But once it became clear the DVD mountain was limited, and there was a much better "online streaming mountain," all of Blockbuster's muscle became a hindrance. It made climbing down increasingly more difficult.

Mere months before filing for bankruptcy, *Fast Company* interviewed Blockbuster's Head of Digital Strategy, Kevin Lewis. Trying to boost confidence around the company's potential, he said, "Never in my wildest dreams would I have aimed this high."[7] I believe he was being honest, but when your Digital Strategy

Officer cannot envision higher heights, you are probably climbing the wrong mountain.

Skin in the Game

Before I co-founded Hetz Ventures, I didn't have much background in venture capital (VC) investing, so I pored over every VC-authored book I could find. In hindsight, I was struck by the difference between the advice in most of these theoretical books and the way things work in practice. In particular, there was one fundamental rule so entrenched in the history of the business; I was shocked to later realize that most venture firms had slowly learned to do the exact opposite.

Here are just a few quotes from some of the industry greats:

"Skin in the game is a critical factor we consider when evaluating entrepreneurs. Founders who have their own personal capital invested in their ventures demonstrate a strong commitment and are more likely to make thoughtful decisions that drive the success of their companies."
    – *Fred Wilson, Co-founder of Union Square Ventures*

"We believe in entrepreneurs who have significant skin in the game because it aligns their interests with ours and creates a stronger partnership. When founders have their own capital at stake, it signals their dedication, accountability, and long-term commitment to building a successful business."
    – *Scott Sandell, Managing General Partner at New Enterprise Associates*

"Having skin in the game is crucial for entrepreneurs because it demonstrates their conviction and willingness to take risks. It shows that they believe in their ideas enough to invest their own resources and take personal responsibility for the outcomes."
    – *Ann Miura-Ko, Co-founder of Floodgate*

"We value entrepreneurs who have skin in the game because it ensures their full commitment and motivation. When founders have their own financial stakes in the success of their companies, they are more likely to persevere through challenges, make difficult decisions, and drive their ventures toward growth."

— Brad Feld, Co-founder of Foundry Group

"Skin in the game is a powerful driver of entrepreneurial success. When founders have their own capital on the line, they have a heightened sense of responsibility and a deeper understanding of the risks involved. It aligns their incentives with ours and fosters a stronger partnership for achieving long-term goals."

— Mary Meeker, Partner at Bond Capital

If "skin in the game" was such a critical factor to success, why were more and more VC investors veering in a different direction? Why were they persuading their entrepreneurs to sell their founder shares to take some money home? The answer: they had too much skin in the game, and it led to a Local Maximum.

Imagine this scenario. A young aspiring entrepreneur, let's call him Jack, raises money from the brutal investors at the fictional Hardnose Capital Fund. Jack does well and builds a business that starts to take off. Meanwhile, Hardnose lives up to its reputation. They force Jack to work at an extremely low salary. He has to eat into his savings and mortgage his house. Even though his business is looking good, and Jack is a millionaire on paper, his day-to-day lifestyle is very challenging.

One day, Google knocks on Jack's door and offers him $120 million for the company. Jack controls his emotions during the meeting, but the moment the Google reps leave his office, he's on the phone to his wife and can't contain his excitement. "This will change our lives," he gushes. "We can pay back our mortgage without any worry. We can finally go on that African safari holiday we've dreamed of. We can send the kids to college, and you can quit your job!"

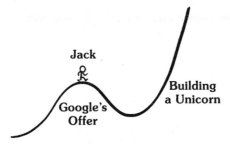

Jack suddenly finds himself at a Local Maximum. By giving up on his long-term dream of building a multi-billion-dollar company, he can now earn a lot of cash, reduce his current stress levels, and enjoy life. Alternatively, he can say no to Google, which will immediately bring him further down the mountain he is on, as he advances toward climbing up the Unicorn Mountain.

Hardnose Capital, on the other hand, sees things differently. Yes, they might make some money on their investment, but $120 million is not enough for the firm's strategy to succeed. They need a much bigger outcome, and they need Jack to continue growing the business. During partner meetings late into the night, they try to devise a strategy to persuade Jack to turn down the offer and build a billion-dollar business. But it's too late for Hardnose Capital. Jack is burned out after years of scraping by, without security for his kids, and the pressures from the bank and at work. The prospect of cashing out and taking some time off is simply too attractive.

Now, imagine a second scenario, one where our founder Jack raised money from fictional Big Outcome Ventures, a firm with a very different approach than Hardnose Capital. Upon investing, Big Outcome Ventures ensured Jack's salary was high enough to cover his ongoing expenses and support his dreams for his family. When Jack's business started doing well, Big Outcome found another investor to buy some of his stock, so he could halve the size of his mortgage. When the Google offer comes through, Jack calls his wife to share the news but he's not sure if he should sell or keep going.

It turns out "skin in the game" is a tactic to ensure that entrepreneurs stay focused on keeping the business viable, and not failing. Skin in the game provides the muscle that will prevent the founder from quitting and pushes him to power through. But having a business "not fail" is not enough. For venture firms to get the huge success stories they need for continued longevity, they have learned to trade off some of that "not fail" muscle in favor of providing entrepreneurs the ability and the agility to say "no" when a big offer comes in. Doing so means going against one of the core commandments of the industry, but it also ultimately helps to avoid getting stuck in a Local Maximum.

Maslow's Hierarchy for Start-ups

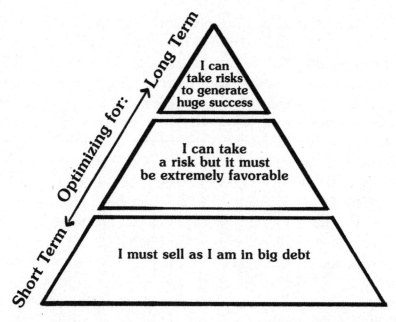

As a founder of a start-up, you may have to trade off the long-term potential of your company with your immediate personal needs. As a result, a founder who is less stressed about money will find it easier to turn down lucrative offers when they believe the business can generate more value. While others, even if they believe in their company, may need to accept early offers and sell.

Survival of the Fittest

By April 2020, at Hetz Ventures, our portfolio's start-up founders were extremely concerned and calling the office daily. It was not because we had something particularly insightful to say or were public health experts. But the COVID-19 pandemic had changed so many of the certainties they had previously relied on. The ability to build and execute business plans under intense uncertainty was being put to a test. Employees had disappeared into quarantine and become remote school substitute teachers for their kids; customer requirements were changing abruptly and in extreme ways, and the outlook on potential future funding was murky, at best. The psychological burden of living during a global pandemic added even more pressure, and it was clear the world would soon look very different.

Looking back – there are obviously outliers – but the number - one indicator of which start-ups benefited, and which ones were hurt by COVID, was their leadership's agility. Executive agility to understand the changing landscape and adjust accordingly was the differentiator between success or failure, far more so than the field they operated in or the amount of cash reserves they had (though both are obviously important). It was not the hefty dinosaurs, but the ants and turtles that survived – not the muscular, but the adaptable. We witnessed travel-tech and property-tech start-ups thrive and healthcare or remote work solutions fail miserably.

In the officers' course in the military, we were forced to memorize a quote by Prussian General Carl Von Clausewitz. It was even engraved on some of the army base walls:

"War is the realm of uncertainty, three quarters of the factors on which action is based are wrapped in a fog of greater or lesser uncertainty."

We were constantly reminded, no matter how much we prepare, study, or memorize, we will quickly find ourselves facing uncertainty, and agility will drive success.

Story after story, we were told that the ability to adapt to new environments is a deciding factor during battle. Case in point: Yom Kippur War hero Brigadier General Avigdor Kahalani was down to his last two tanks, neither of which even had ammunition. By driving those two tanks around in circles, he managed to create the illusion of a full brigade. His tactic was effective to the degree it caused the Syrians to retreat. And when paratroopers couldn't penetrate the Jordanian defense lines during the Independence War in 1948, they brought in a secret weapon – Davidka[8] – a machine that made such a loud and terrifying sound it caused soldiers and civilians to run away in fear.

It may be hard to teach agility, but it is both a value that can be embedded and a skill that can be trained. More often than not, our military assignments, missions, and drills intentionally included a twist that forced us to think in an agile way. Although we did not expect a three-minute extension during our sand hole digging competition, and it had never happened before, the notion of change was not foreign to anyone, and we were prepared to adapt.

In the start-up world, the notion of agility is constantly coming into play as well. Founders are told to keep moving, to stay agile. The ability to do so is a clear advantage over larger, older, chunkier organizations. Blockbuster's muscly heft rendered it immobile in the face of Netflix, a swiftly swimming agile start-up. The idea of building muscle is appealing, whether in front of the mirror at the gym or as an organization deepening its capabilities and operations. It turns out, however, agility is no less important, and sometimes even more so, in rapidly changing and unpredictable environments. We must therefore learn to ask ourselves, and the organizations we operate, whether we are widening our sand holes as much as we are deepening them.

A Little Byte of Data Science

Neural networks, or "deep learning algorithms," are at the heart of technologies such as ChatGPT, machine vision, and many others. Even to the most experienced developers, they feel like dark magic, because nobody fully understands how they work or is able to explain each individual outcome. The developers of these networks have to constantly trade off between agility and muscle, or how deep and how wide their networks should be. The networks can be trained on anything – text, mortgages, images, code, virtually anything the human mind can conceive – and the results it spits out are ridiculously good. And, over time, we are consistently learning the flexible/agile networks are outperforming the muscular ones.

Typically, a neural network is categorized according to the number of layers it contains (this reflects its depth, and it is also where the term "deep learning" originates) and the number of neurons/variables in each layer (this reflects its width). Simply put, the number of layers typically correlates with the "muscle," while the number of neurons in each layer reflects how agile it is. The input layer is where it collects information. In machine vision, this could be the colors and shapes of a picture. The output layer provides the answer the algorithm believes to be correct. For example, machine vision software responds "cat" if it believes the image is of a cat. Between the input and the output layers, there are many more hidden layers where the algorithm does its computation. (Unlike in normal algorithms, where there is one computation, here each hidden layer takes the output from the layer before it does a computation and provides the input to the layer after it.)

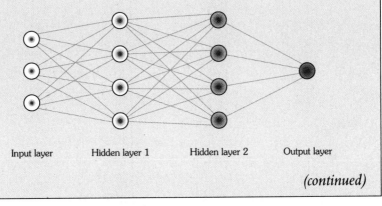

Input layer   Hidden layer 1   Hidden layer 2   Output layer

(continued)

(continued)

Interestingly, the results consistently favor breadth over depth. Data scientists find neural networks that are too deep in comparison to their width are stiff, don't adapt fast enough, and underperform over longer periods of time. See the way the leading OpenAI scientists built GPT-1, GPT-2, and GPT-3.

	GPT-1	GPT-2	GPT-3
layers	12	48	96
neurons	117M	1.5B	175B

Notice how many millions (and billions) of neurons the scientists have accounted for in only a few layers.

Chapter 5

The Mountain Within – The Psychology of a Local Maximum

Once an idea has taken hold of the brain, it's almost impossible to eradicate.
— Leonardo DiCaprio, as Dom Cobb in *Inception* (2010)

Most of the extensive training and drills required to become a paratrooper take place in the desert, including night navigation. As the name suggests, each soldier is challenged to navigate alone, without a map, on a moonless night, and let me tell you, it can get pretty scary out there. We're fully aware of the myriad dangers and the wild, nocturnal animals we're sure to encounter. But getting lost is the biggest fear. We spent a good part of the previous day carefully studying our individual navigation routes, trying to identify different "anchors" along the way to help us keep track of our whereabouts: a clump of trees, a meeting of valleys, the bottom of a ridge, etc. Nerves were running extra high because we'd all heard the story about the guy who got lost and fell off a cliff to his death during the night navigation drill, and no one was eager to meet the same fate. After being tested by the group commanders on our knowledge of our routes, we checked our equipment, filled our water bottles, and, with our adrenaline pumping, the race was on.

Our leaving times were staggered, and we set off in our own directions. Our commander was in his Jeep with a driver, who was mapping where we were supposed to be at every stage throughout the night. Knowing he had a surveillance system didn't diminish the strange exhilaration of walking alone in complete silence for hours. But there were challenges every step of the way. We were equipped with a communication device, only to be used when we reached the agreed upon landmarks along the way (typically, every 10 to 15 kilometers) or once an hour to briefly touch base. There was a third occasion when the device could be used, though we would be embarrassed to do so, which was if we got lost and had given up hope of recovering our bearings.

The terrain was difficult and the visibility poor. Although I felt in control, I was surprised by the wave of relief that swept over me when I finally saw the commander's Jeep parked behind a dune. I removed my equipment, drenched with sweat, and sat down next to the few soldiers who finished before me. These were fun times, and we enjoyed a cup of steaming Turkish coffee as we waited for the others. An hour passed, and a few more joined us. Two hours passed, and we assessed who had yet to trickle in. We were approaching 3 a.m., which was the hard cutoff. After this, any arrivals would be considered to have failed.

Another soldier, Dov, came running up to our huddle, exhausted, yet nevertheless on time. But where was Uri? Not one to botch an exercise, Uri was meticulous, thorough, and driven by a strong set of values. Tall and confident, he's known for taking hard hits during our Krav Maga sessions and carrying on without complaint. He joined our unit after dropping out of the Air Force, and service is in his blood. He dreamed of becoming a doctor and living in a house he built with his own hands. But where the hell was he?

We stopped chatting to listen in on the conversation happening in the Jeep. Our commander opened communication with Uri and asked him to report his whereabouts. "Two miles from the finish line, should be there in 15 min," we heard Uri's voice reply. Thirty minutes later, the commander, spoke firmly into the encrypted communication device and demanded to know Uri's exact location. "30 degrees from the river bend, and 130 degrees from the peak of mountain 408. I will be with you in 5 minutes," we heard Uri say.

For fifteen minutes, we sat silently praying Uri would show up, but nothing. The commander was clearly aggravated and possibly a little nervous himself. He ordered Uri to open his map, remove the flashlight sealed in his backpack for emergencies, find his bearings, and report back. After a minute of silence, we heard Uri say, "I can see where I went wrong. I will be with you in 40 minutes."

Uri sounded like he knew what he was doing and where he was, but the commander's attuned senses told him something was wrong. Uri's apparent confidence only increased the commander's concern. Using a tactic known as *Imutim* (translation: proofs, or verifications) to track his hunch that Uri's mind was playing tricks on him, the commander ordered Uri to report in every 10 minutes and verbally communicate what he saw and what he expected to see in 10 minutes' time. The use of *Imutim* was intended to gradually force Uri's mind to reconcile with what he saw with his eyes. The idea was to locate markers that caused him to question how sure he was.

We listened anxiously to each of Uri's 10-minute staggered reports:

"I see a narrow valley sloping downwards and three hilltops on my right. I expect to reach the bottom of this valley and see a track that bends to my left at the bottom."

"I see a path that continues straight and then bears to the right, with three mountains still to my right. I expect to soon see a village in the distance 240 degrees from north."

"I see a village 200 degrees north and expect the path to soon bear right."

Despite careful monitoring, Uri's responses didn't quite add up. He was committed to believing he was heading in the right direction. After an hour of communicating in this manner, the commander ordered Uri to fire his flare. Another two Jeeps joined us in case we needed to set off in search of a missing soldier. We were instructed to climb onto a hill and scout the landscape for Uri's flare. And sure enough, about 15 miles away and clearly well-off course, we saw the green sparks of his flair. The Jeeps raced toward it, and 90 minutes later, Uri joined the group.

Later that night, we finally heard from Uri what had happened. "I really wanted to do well, and I actually think I was doing well at the beginning. But the visibility wasn't good, and I started fitting reality around me to what I was expecting to see. I remembered a mountain straight ahead, and in practice, it was sort of straight ahead, but not quite, so I just made it work. Gradually, I fit reality to my memorized path and just kept going. Even when I opened the map and worked with the commander, it didn't help! At one point, I thought the path was turning right, but now looking back, I can tell I was just walking straight."

Uri hadn't been hiking the same terrain as us. He'd been hiking a terrain constructed by his own imagination. Often, the most significant constraints are the ones within our own minds.

Overcoming Confirmation Bias

Uri's ordeal in the desert is a striking example of the human tendency to bend our perception of reality to fit our preconceptions, also known as "confirmation bias." Rather than questioning what he saw, Uri's internal narrative was repeatedly reinforced by new information he interpreted to back it up. We all do this.

Regardless of which side of the political sphere you are on, you're more likely to view a major event as confirmation of your belief than one that challenges it. For example, a shooting in America leads both sides of the political spectrum to see their arguments confirmed by the event. In his book *The Righteous*

Mind: Why Good People Are Divided by Politics and Religion,[1] Jonathan Haidt argues that our moral judgments aren't based on rationalization or reflection, but on intuition and gut feelings. Logical arguments and rational thoughts, Haidt says, are often used to justify our initial reactions. So ingrained are our internal biases, we are more likely to interpret and even remember events we saw with our own eyes differently than we are to adapt our views and understanding to reality.

The human tendency to create echo chambers, by surrounding ourselves with people and information that support our preconceptions rather than challenge them, directly tilts us toward Local Maximums. In fact, this tendency leads to the exact opposite of A/B/X testing. Rather than considering alternative and potentially far better paths, our brains close off access to those paths entirely. Extreme cases of confirmation bias eliminate even A/B testing in favor of simply A (non)testing: there is only one path, and only information that reinforces it slips through our filters. This scenario is far more problematic than simply being at a suboptimal point, as our mind paints the entire field around us differently.

Dov, the soldier who reached the Jeep just before the 3 a.m. cutoff time, admitted to us that he realized he was somewhat lost during the exercise. He sensed his surroundings didn't quite fit what he expected. About halfway into the navigation, Dov started a process called *Nesher* (translation: eagle). Every few miles, he hiked to the top of a mountain to review his surroundings and make sure he hadn't drifted off track. His approach wasn't optimal, as it was both slow and tiring, but he was aware of his situation and figured, given his options, situational awareness was better than being lost. Uri, on the other hand, believed he was on the very best, optimal route, and he kept reinforcing that belief with every misstep.

Start-up founders are particularly prone to finding themselves in a Local Maximum as a result of confirmation bias. These individuals tend to be naturally optimistic (who else voluntarily embarks on a blood-sweat-tears-fueled journey of starting a company?) and work around the clock to make their game-changing vision a reality. Most of their days are an uphill challenge. When something happens that is even remotely related to their desired outcome, it can be tempting (often unconsciously) to interpret that information as supportive of their goal.

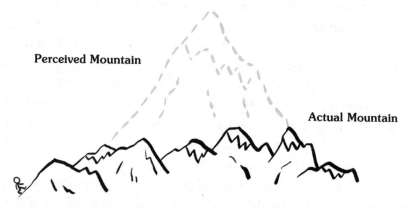

Perceived Mountain

Actual Mountain

Often, we imagine the mountain we face is much more attractive than it is in reality. Start-up founders pitch their ideas and sometimes hear what they would like to hear to paint a picture that the potential of their venture is far better than it is in practice.

At our venture firm, asking entrepreneurs to summarize their key takeaways from conversations with industry experts has proven to be a revealing technique. It helps us predict which founders are likely to navigate their companies to more optimal elevations and which will keep digging in their heels. When we compare the advice given by the industry expert with a read-out of the conversation reported by the founder, we often discover that what he or she heard is very different from what was actually said. For example, the expert might have said, "I have seen many start-ups in this space. While you are doing something different, it is still going to be really hard." Yet, the founder heard, "It's a hard space, and he has seen many start-ups doing what we're doing, but he thinks we are different." The founder hears what he wants to hear, and this is quite common.

Learning to listen accurately is not the only way to avoid the echo chambers that lead to a Local Maximum. Learning to ask questions correctly is equally as important. In his book, *The Mom Test*,[2] Rob Fitzpatrick highlights the value of asking questions that lead to insightful answers, rather than asking questions that provoke flattering answers of little use. He argues it is possible to craft questions in a manner that even your mother will provide useful insights to versus simple flattery, by asking open questions instead of closed ones. "Mom, I spent my whole summer holiday inventing this new coffee cup. Do you think it's cool?" is likely to lead to a meaningless answer. Whereas, "Mom, what are the main features you look for in a coffee cup, and which of those features are better or worse with this one?" will lead to greater insight.

Asking insightful, open questions is something computers strive to do better, too. Although machine learning algorithms continuously improve as more data is fed into the system, the rate at which they improve heavily depends on the variance of the dataset. In other words, algorithms have learned that echo chambers make them less accurate and can be misleading.

For example, if you want to teach an algorithm to read an ultrasound, feeding it relatively similar scans – say, from a certain angle, resolution, or of certain types of people – will only get you so far. Gradually, the machine's capabilities will plateau unless it is fed data of a different nature. In data science, methodologies are continually being developed and improved to address such biases. Today, there are software systems that will tell you what type of data your algorithms are missing to make them more robust. In the case of our ultrasound reading algorithm, the system may say it requires more examples, perhaps specifically of children, where the ultrasound looked positive (showing white dots in key areas), but the full diagnoses still turned out to be negative.

Another machine learning technique is called "Random Forest,"[3] invented by Leo Breiman and Adele Cutler in the early 2000s. Leo Breiman, a prominent statistician and professor at the

University of California, Berkeley, introduced the Random Forest algorithm to try to address "overfitting," an overly narrow approach to problem solving. Unlike typical decision-making trees, instead of taking one path that might lead to getting stuck or overfitting a solution into a Local Maximum, Random Forest incorporates multiple viewpoints (decision-making trees) to reach a better conclusion.

Let's say you're information gathering about Jonathan, a guest at a charity you're involved in. You want to determine how wealthy he is and have the opportunity to question an acquaintance who knows him well. A typical decision tree with four layers (meaning four questions) might work like this:

You: Does he have a job?
Acquaintance: No.
You: Did he have a job in the last five years?
(*You wouldn't ask this question if he had said "yes." You would ask a different one.)
Acquaintance: No.
You: Is he looking for a job?
Acquaintance: No.
You: Did he ever have a job?
Acquaintance: Yes.

Now, close your eyes and guess how much money Jonathan has in his bank account. Did you assume the guy's barely making it? What if he happens to be a multi-millionaire? Where did you go wrong? Your decision tree was a good one, but it relied on the fact that Jonathan's wealth depended on a job. A different sequence of questions could have focused on inheritance.

- Are both of his parents living?
- Did he inherit money from a family member?
- Was the family member someone with multiple assets worth millions of dollars?
- How many people received part of this wealth?

Alternatively, you could have built a decision tree around the assumption that Jonathan gained wealth through stocks or the sale of an asset.

- Did he ever run a business?
- How many people worked for him?
- What was the company's turnover?
- Did he sell the business?

Finally, you could have built a decision tree around Jonathan's spend, assuming it closely corresponds with his wealth.

- Does he own a home?
- Is this the only home that he own?
- How many times a year do he travel?
- What class does he fly?

Random Forest is unique as it uses a set of algorithms that run many scenarios, such as all four of the above examples in parallel. At the end, it normalizes the responses across categories. For example, I could have gotten a low-wealth suggestion on three of the four decision trees, but one of them strongly indicated that Jonathan sold his company for huge sums of money. He enjoys a simple life of volunteering versus taking extravagant vacations multiple times a year, and the other decision trees didn't catch this. Data scientists use the terminology of "choosing the wrong tree." In this book, our terminology is "climbing the wrong mountain."

Asking the correct questions and/or employing a Random Forest technique are far more than algorithmic safeguards; they can lead us away from the dangerous echo chambers that lead to Local Maximums. A variance of data, as explored through the ultrasound example, and the consideration of multiple viewpoints, as explored through Random Forest, reflect a broad and wide encompassing perspective we should cultivate both in our own minds and in our organizations. This perspective doesn't close us off from the paths that might potentially disrupt our assumptions.

Rather, it actively seeks those paths out, so we may refine and improve our assumptions.

Trapped by the Mental Output Gap

Our mental beliefs and assumptions don't just affect the way we interpret reality; they affect our performance. Once we have latched onto a particular concept, our behavior will adapt to conform to it.

In military try-outs, 17-year-olds arrive on a stretch of sand dunes and are divided into groups of 20. Throughout the day, they compete against each other in a variety of physical tasks: sprints, crawls, sandbag carrying, digging holes. All of the participants start the day with the hope of being selected to join an elite combat unit.

Ezra, a leading military psychologist, explained the mental Local Maximum the cadets face: "A common saying amongst Israeli youngsters preparing for the army is: 'It's all in your head.' And while they are right in theory, in practice, they miss the point. They believe the main mental challenge is to push themselves further, run a bit faster, or do that extra push-up. In reality, we see the main challenge is the mental one they face within themselves. When we analyze the results from all the different groups and exercises, we see something odd," notes Ezra. "Within literally the first 15 to 20 minutes of the entire day, each of the 20 individuals will have found their position within their group, and it will rarely change again throughout the rest of the day. Whoever placed fourth in the first three sprints will likely stay fourth, even 50 sprints later."

Physically, this trend does not make sense; some people are naturally better at one or two sprints while others are better at performing many sprints. But mentally, people position themselves within their group and act accordingly. As Ezra further explains, "When running exercises, we've learned a Number Four will give up quickly when paired against Number Three. He has mentally positioned himself below Number Three, and yet, he will fight hard when competing against Number Five. It seems that, within just a few minutes of meeting each other and starting an exercise, an unofficial status quo of positions is created. Amazingly, this holds true throughout the day and across different tasks. Very few of the cadets are willing to challenge their position and move up."

So, yes, "it's all in your head" rings true when the cadet's biggest challenge is to contest the group's agreed-upon maximum. This is obviously good news if you happen to be first or second in the group, but those further down the rankings get put into a mental Local Maximum. They believe they are at their peak and cannot go any higher or do any better. As a result, and without realizing this Local Maximum is increasingly harder to break out of, it eventually fulfills itself. The best tip for these aspiring commandos is to go all out at the beginning. Put yourself on the tallest mountain.

Teenagers running in ranked sprints during military tryouts are not the only ones who get stuck in their own mental maximums: we all do it. Many of us are so trapped in our internal landscapes, we're not even aware of it.

Philip, a start-up founder we invested in, utilized the human tendency to latch onto mental maximums to his benefit. He was in the process of launching a company in the machine learning space. As is customary, he booked a trip to Silicon Valley to drum up interest and hopefully, customers. The last thing anyone wants is to be harassed by some no-name Israeli entrepreneur claiming to have the "next best thing in AI." Those guys get millions of such calls a year, and Philip was having a very hard time getting anyone to take a meeting with him. So, he came up with a unique strategy and created a group of the best and brightest senior AI practitioners. He made it exclusive by requiring that everyone submit a CV and endure a rigorous selection process to be accepted. He even created an entrance exam. Soon, word got out around Silicon Valley about his group, and sure enough, people were clamoring to be part of it. Within three weeks some of the top developers who wouldn't meet with him initially were banging down the door to get in. Philip, strategically, accepted only a small handful of them to make the others want in even more. His plan worked, and when it was time for him to present his machine learning concept, he had the top 50 in attendance to hear his fireside chat. We tend to think that the harder something is, the better it is. Philip created the illusion of a high mountain, and suddenly, everyone wanted to climb it.

Sometimes, we get so fixated on what we think we're supposed to do, we don't stop to consider any other alternative. One time, when I was visiting Manhattan, I went into a pizza shop. It was a typical family-run restaurant owned by an Italian immigrant. Most of the employees were his children, cousins, and extended family who were all shouting orders at each other in Italian. It was a lively scene, and I got a kick out of it, but there was just one problem: the pizza. It was awful, and it seemed I wasn't the only one who thought so, as the shop was nearly empty. On the other hand, the juices were great. I sat there for a Zoom call and noticed that customers came in, ordered a juice, and left. As I was heading out, I thanked the owner and asked him if he had considered focusing on selling juice instead of pizza. "Juice?!" he said, surprised, and looking at me like I was nuts. "We are Italian, we sell pizza!"

In economic terms, an output gap is the difference between what an economy can potentially produce and what it actually does produce. A "mental output gap" is the difference between what we believe we can achieve and what we actually can achieve. Yes, some people believe they can achieve more than they actually can, but most of us simply get used to a certain outcome in our daily lives and don't expect much more of ourselves.

Takala, from Tech-Career, told me that in the early years of the program, the graduates' salaries weren't fixed in advance, meaning they negotiated their own terms for their first jobs. "It was infuriating," he recalled, "These were our top graduates, who scored extremely high on the application tests, and they agreed to ridiculously basic salaries. As soon as they walked into the room to negotiate their contract terms, it's like they forgot they aced the test and were in high demand. And the worst part was they thought they aced the negotiations!"

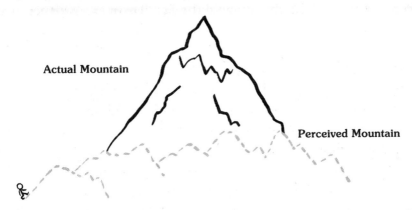

Actual Mountain

Perceived Mountain

Periodically, we belittle the mountain ahead and believe the opportunity is far smaller than it is in reality. We get used to a steady state, such as the young sprinters in military tryouts, pizza shop owners who are psychologically trapped by their Italian roots, or Takala's graduates who don't think about asking for a higher salary.

These types of mental output gaps are painful to witness, and they are hard to let go of, too. Just ask a monkey.

In South India, monkeys were a huge pest to the local villagers, and they were constantly nicking items from the markets and helping themselves to anything they could get their hands on. Fed up with the harassment, the locals developed an ingenious way of trapping them. The trap consists of a hollowed-out coconut, chained to a stake and filled with rice,[4] accessible through a small hole. Crucially, the hole is just big enough for the monkey's hand to go in, but too small for his fist clenched with rice to come out. The monkey reaches in, grabs the rice, and is suddenly trapped. He realizes he is in trouble, and he screams and shouts but will not let go of the rice. There is nothing preventing him from freeing himself from the trap, but it doesn't occur to him to unclench his fist, even as the local villagers draw in closer and closer to capture him. He's not physically trapped; he's mentally trapped by a false notion (that he is trapped)!

We may smirk at the monkey's stupidity, but often we are hardly any different ourselves, unable to let go of the conceptions that keep us trapped in a Local Maximum. An example of this can be found in military shipbuilding. In the first half of the 20th century, control of the sea equated to holding an ace of victory for winning wars. The correlation was so strong, that more and more focus was given to building bigger and better warships. Newer versions of ships typically included more guns and more armor. Generals, hungry for firepower, measured the ships' capabilities by the number of guns and tons of armor on board. It took the independent thinking Admiral Jacky Fisher to think outside the coconut and realize that this approach was locking navies into suboptimal thinking. The *Dreadnought*, with fewer guns and less armor but more strategically placed, was just as lethal but far more agile and maneuverable. When reviewing the performance of his new ship Fisher famously said: "Fear God and Dread Nought."

We, like the monkeys, couldn't quite bring ourselves to let go. Instead of being trapped by a fistful of rice, we became trapped by our extra guns and armor. In the attempt to arm and protect ourselves, we made ourselves weaker in the face of our enemies.

We see this same tendency play out in the innovation space all the time. For example, as newer models of the iPhone are rolled out, the developers must ask themselves, "What's not working? What can we do without?" Maybe the newer models need fewer features and functionalities instead of more? Similar to the shipbuilders who tried to rule the sea by building bigger and better ships, sometimes the best solution is to scale back instead of to add more.

We are all monkeys, battling our mental gaps and the hunger for more – more rice in our paws, more guns on our ships, and more apps on our phones.

Maybe the Opposite Is Right

These examples come to remind us that often our minds are our biggest enemies. We tend to reinforce our current beliefs, distorting our understanding of the landscape and sending us toward mountain peaks that simply don't exist, like Uri. Other times, we lack the belief that we can do better, letting those around us or our own self-perception place us in a mental Local Maximum, like the new recruits in the military, the Italian pizza shop owner in New York, or Takala's early graduates. We believe we are at the peak, but we are actually far from it. These mental habits are some of the hardest to break, as they require us to question beliefs we have come to rely on.

In 1973, contrary to the Israeli intelligence agency's firmly held assumptions, Israel was taken by deadly surprise by Syria and Egypt on the sacred Jewish holiday of Yom Kippur. The battle was one of the toughest and costliest in Israel's history, and the fallout was swift. Prime Minister Golda Meir resigned, the head of the IDF intelligence had a bitter public dispute with the head of the Mossad, and the status of IDF officers was severely damaged.

In the aftermath of the attack, many faults and miscalculations became apparent although one seemed to underscore the rest. The senior generals created a narrative around why Syrian and Egyptian militaries were amassing on the borders, and no information could change this narrative. Meanwhile, the intelligence generals, who were trained at calibrating information, kept fitting the new information into their current beliefs: there wouldn't be an attack. Junior IDF officers were convinced the attack was imminent, but the more senior staff were wedded to increasingly elaborate explanations as to why particular events were unfolding. Soldiers on the border? They were preparing for a drill. Large forces and tanks being called up? Nasser needed to make a show of strength. Calls for the imminent destruction of Israel? This is fairly normal hate speech and occurs all the time, so why should it be any different this time?

Today, when the story of the Yom Kippur War is retold in Officer's School, they call it, "The Conception." How has the military developed since 1973 to protect itself from a similar conception in the future? In short: *Ipcha Mistabra*.

Ipcha Mistabra is an Aramaic term used throughout the Talmud. Literally translated, it means, "maybe the opposite is right." In 200 CE, Talmud rabbis debated different scenarios and questioned every possibility only to find the most obscure examples to contradict well-established truths. While doing so, these rabbis would stop at no end to prove each other wrong. They used the term *Ipcha Mistabra* when they could build a contradictory logic that still held true with the same facts. Through a Local Maximum lens, we can understand the rabbis' approach: they were testing other paths to make sure the one they were climbing was the best.

In modern day times, the phrase is used for less weighty debates. For example, your child announces the garden furniture is wet. You immediately assume your neighbor has poured his dirty water over the balcony onto your porch, yet again. Your wife challenges this logic and says, "*Ipcha Mistabra*, it may have rained last night and that's why the furniture is wet."

As a result of the terrible intelligence failure that led to the Yom Kippur War, the military didn't automatically conclude it needed more soldiers on standby. It didn't come out with a statement saying, "In the future, if there's any doubt, we will call in the reserves." Both of these outcomes would have been tremendously expensive and would have failed to address the core of the problem. When your mindset is in a Local Maximum, the entire field is distorted; Israel may have called in the reserves but used them incorrectly, positioned them wrongly, or simply not prepared the logistical infrastructure required for the approaching war. Recognizing the potential for catastrophic results, the military had to change a fundamental aspect of its thinking to hopefully allow it to understand its surroundings more accurately in the future.

In 1974, the Israeli military implemented two new processes to facilitate such goals based upon *Ipcha Mistabra*. First, they created a new unit named Ipcha Mistabra, which receives access to any information it desires, with the goal of challenging any assumptions the broader intelligence may have. Second, they stated that any soldier is allowed to write a report and argue against the current intelligence beliefs. They can challenge the assumptions of his or her superiors without fear of repercussion. The report must be shared with at least one person who is a rank above the report writer's commanding officer. The *Ipcha Mistabra* system is designed to allow for the facts to be organized differently and to implement ongoing checks to ensure the intelligence community understands the playing field correctly.

Since its inception, *Ipcha Mistabras* have been written on a broad array of topics: why an intelligence operation will not succeed, will there or won't there be an attack, an agent is a double agent, a system will fail in time of war, a transit doesn't carry the expected equipment, and many more. It should be stressed *Ipcha Mistabra* is not a mechanism for proposing a specific course of action (such as developing a system that detects tunnels or launching a preliminary strike); it is a method that puts our current understanding of the environment around us to the test.

Following the horrific atrocities on October 7, 2023, an inquiry has been commissioned. As this is ongoing, and the book is being written as events unfold, one truth is clear: there was a huge misconception. By October 8, many citizens had already asked where the *Ipcha Mistabra* was, and by November, a leading ex-general reported that the organizational *Ipcha Mistabra* was buried within the layered organization. As the IDF has regrettably learned the hard way, these skills must be not only acquired, but constantly sharpened, refined, and reinforced. We have found that *Ipcha Mistabra*, like many of the techniques to avoid a Local Maximum, is a muscle that needs to be continuously exercised.

Reality Check

Sometimes, we continue on the wrong path (even though we know it's wrong) simply because we can't accept the alternative. When we see a mountain or a ridge instead of a peak, be aware that our mental beliefs have likely distorted our understanding of the information in front of us. We may unconsciously reimagine the landscape to fit our preconceptions, as Uri did during the night navigation exercise. Very often, our confidence is our greatest weakness.

For many years, I coached junior school soccer teams, and discovered that among the young players there were broadly three types of players. There are the ones who are not particularly good and don't really care about winning, but they have a great time just kicking the ball around and having fun. Then, there are the players who are quite good. They're used to winning, which often means they're also sore losers. Sometimes, their desire to win gives them the extra drive on the field but when they don't win, they blame everyone else for the loss. The third type of players is the very best. They're the ones who, over the course of the year, demonstrate their ability to truly excel, and they are also harder on themselves than they are on their teammates. They don't look for external excuses; they are honest with their results, which allow them to reach higher peaks. As Michael Jordan put it: "Accept a loss as a learning experience, and never point fingers at your teammates." The notion that "we are right" or "we are the best" can be powerful, but it can also lead us astray, especially when we think we're in one place, but it turns out we're in another.

Unfortunately, we do this more often than we think, sometimes with long-lasting effects. Think about the internal dialogue that often accompanies confidence: My boss loves me, and I'm going to get a promotion next quarter. I'm climbing the tallest mountain, and I'm going to beat everyone else to the top. I'm Italian, and people love my pizza. This type of thinking can be rooted in a company culture as well, from start-ups to large corporations.

There's an old joke about a man who attempted to train his donkey to eat less. Every day, he provided it with slightly less food than the day before. And one day, the donkey didn't wake up. "What a shame," the man said, "if he had only lived a little longer, I could have taught him to not eat at all!" While the joke may or may not be funny, clearly the man tells this story because he doesn't want to admit the truth: he killed his own donkey.

When "knowing" something definitively takes hold, it's time for a reality check, which can be accomplished through Pre-Mortem, a method of risk assessment, developed by cognitive psychologist

Gary Klein in 2007.[5] His technique suggests working backward from the point of failure to find a solution. Similar to *Ipcha Mistabra*, Pre-Mortem is an organizational procedure that gives voice to the nagging questions we might otherwise ignore. Different than *Ipcha Mistabra*, a Pre-Mortem doesn't ask what could be wrong with your plan or current understanding of a situation, but dictates that we acknowledge the plan failed and ask how could this have happened.

Say you are about to launch a new business. Rather than questioning where the weak points are in your current plan, a Pre-Mortem asks you to imagine: "In three years, your business will fail, and you will be forced to shut down. Why? What went wrong?" Looking into the future to analyze potential failure points is an effective strategy to identify weak spots. Weaknesses can be overcome. Perhaps there's an issue or bug with the product. Perhaps you misjudged the price point or your go-to-market plan. A Pre-Mortem can reveal risks you might not otherwise be aware of so you can prepare for them. For example, a crucial team member leaves, a large competitor offers a similar product for free, or a key supplier goes bust. Any one of these scenarios can derail a business to the point of no return.

As Klein demonstrates, running a thought experiment that dictates the outcome as a failure allows our perspective to shift so that we may question our beliefs and examine the underlying assumptions we hold to be true. By unlocking our ability to view the different outcomes and the potential paths to them, we allow ourselves to recognize and even steer away from unwanted outcomes and Local Maximum traps.

Pre-Mortem, *Imutim*, Random Forest, *Nesher*, and *Ipcha Mistabra* are effective techniques to avoid the mirage in the desert, the seduction of the "tallest" mountain peak, or our own overconfident beliefs in our guaranteed success. They help us to challenge the inner confidence that can lead us down a misguided and even dangerous path. To ensure we are not caught in a trap, be it by a real enemy combatant or our own powerful mental enemies, we need to build checks into our thinking to balance psychological perceptions with reality.

A Little Byte of Data Science

People are afraid AI is going to take over the world, and we'll all be living in some sort of post-apocalyptic, robot-dominated reality. Data scientists and developers typically do not share this fear but there is a concern that AI can go astray. While software algorithms don't have psychological barriers, they do have similar challenges. Just like humans, a key obstacle for any algorithm is a misleading "belief" that can limit its potential.

The Israeli Navy's recruitment team is extremely proud of the fact that they are "data driven" when identifying and selecting candidates for the intensive Navy Seal training program. Out of thousands of applicants, only 2% start the program, and only two dozen finish. Software models predict which candidates are most likely to graduate. These models include a wide array of variables: psychological analysis, fitness, coordination, arithmetic, stamina, and many more. Every year, a data science team further refines the models to continue improving their predictive abilities, and especially, to determine how much weight to give each variable.

One year, a data scientist questioned why geographic location (or, where the candidate lived) was given so much weight and suggested potentially eliminating the variable. "Why should this matter?" he rationalized. His superiors told him they are "data-driven," and the data suggested this variable was actually one of the best predictors of them all.

After some persistence from the data scientist, they ran a test for the model without the "hometown" variable and were astonished to discover the algorithm dramatically improved. It turns out, cadets who wanted to be Navy Seals often move closer to the sea, and more specifically, to neighborhoods near the Seals base. However, cadets who did not live near the sea or the Seals had just as much chance of succeeding as those who did. The data system was biased against those cadets.

Google, Amazon, Facebook, Apple, and all the big tech companies fear the variables (or shall I say, "beliefs") that lead to a Local Maximum. One growing concern is that the data initially used to train the models was misleading and, therefore, the algorithm continues to learn, but with a glaring problematic variable. For example, if I train an insurance algorithm on a huge amount of data from 2020, the dataset might be enormous and seem robust. But omitting that Covid occurred that year would send my algorithm into a frenzy. I would predict very few tourism claims (without knowing that year had very few tourists) and a huge percentage of hospitalizations. Premium costs would be terrible. Similarly, if Amazon retrained its models in December of each year to predict the following year's online shopping volume, think how inaccurate the predictions would be if they assumed Christmas shopping levels for January through November.

The common fear is of basing our beliefs on something that turns out to be wrong, knowingly or not. To reduce the danger this can pose, computer scientists stress test their models constantly. They build *Ipcha Mistabras* into their algorithms, so the model keeps asking itself: Could there be another way to explain what it sees?

Chapter 6

Time: The Fourth Dimension

Time is a dressmaker specializing in alterations.

— Confucius

During officers' course, we were navigating, once again, in the Negev desert. The core theme of the week was learning to accurately estimate how long different drills would take. Again and again, we were told stories of commanders who managed to execute their mission only to find they got the timing wrong: the terrorists escaped, targets were missed, or the combat teams were ambushed. "If your timing is off, everything else is irrelevant," we were told.

After a routine navigation drill, we were gathered at the bottom of a sand dune to debrief in advance of the night navigational exercise. Instead of giving us the usual topographic maps to strategize which route to take and memorize key points along the way, the head officer hit us with a surprise. He divided us into six groups of eight and dropped 200 drinking straws (yes, drinking straws, the plastic ones) in the middle of each group.

Deadpan, he announced: "You are on a failed top-secret mission. You are now stuck deep inside of Syria. Drones are circling at an altitude of 30,000 feet waiting to receive your location signal so a rescue mission can be sent. To send the signal, you must construct the tallest antenna possible using these 200 straws. The group with tallest antenna wins a weekend off at home with your families. You've got one hour, 60 minutes. GO."

A weekend at home was huge! Our group swiftly appointed a leader, as we had learned that having a single decision point eliminates friction and increases efficiency. We had a brief brainstorming session, reviewed a variety of proposed antenna shapes, and decided to go with a triangular construction. In theory, it sounded smart. A triangle wouldn't wobble like a square, and it required fewer straws for each level, which allowed us to build taller.

Confident with our plan, we started squeezing the straw ends into each other for our triangular assembly. Unfortunately, we quickly saw the difference between our theoretical tall straw tower and the pile of flimsy straws lying in the sand. It was pointless. Triangular, square, or any other shape: no straw tower was going to be able to withstand the open desert wind. A quick look at our watches showed we had just wasted over 20 minutes.

Back to the drawing board, or should I say, sand board. We sat there, staring at the straws in a pathetic pile, anchored by a stone to prevent them from blowing away. Clearly, we would need to use elements from our surroundings to stabilize our straw antenna. The pressure was on. We noticed one team scurrying to collect large rocks and another team scooping up branches. Time was ticking against us, and the available resources were shrinking. Luckily, we had Doron.

Doron viewed problems in an unusual way. He was a trained aeronautics engineer with a master's in physics, and he often suggested ideas that pushed the limits of the guidelines we were given. Once, we were told to stand in lines of three. Someone was standing slightly out of line, which threw off the symmetry of our placement. Doron explained to the macho infantry officer that if he were to stand on a ladder, fifty yards diagonal to where we were standing, it would appear as if we were in symmetric, three-by-three lines. The officer was baffled. Another time, during "battle week," we simulated being at war with limited food and water. During a navigation drill, Doron found a shepherd who was willing to exchange one of his sheep for some of our bullets. Needless to say, our officers were furious when he returned to camp that night with a sheep but short of a few bullets. (The funny part was, Doron was fuming. He thought his solution was well within the parameters we'd been given.)

Looking around at the straws and the other teams, Doron noticed the senior officer (who was running the exercise) had arrived by Jeep. Being an Army-grade Jeep, it had a very long antenna on the roof. "Why don't we simply connect the straws to the officer's antenna? We can fasten one straw at the top and let the rest drop the whole way down to the sand." We stared at each other. Was this even allowed? A quick debate erupted, but with the time ticking against us and the other teams making progress, Doron got his way. We were back to sticking straws into each other, only this time, with the purpose of making one long straw we could dangle down from the Jeep's antenna.

Six groups of officer cadets worked furiously against the clock to execute on their own antenna building strategies. Two teams were using rocks, one was using branches, one was using their guns to build a tower, one team seemed to be cluelessly connecting all their straws together in one extremely long line, and then there was us, the Jeep team. As time raced by, we gained confidence. The Jeep's antenna was about 6 feet long, and the height of the roof added another 4 to 5 feet. We could feel the sweet victory of a weekend at home within our grasp.

Our team finished with a good five minutes to spare. We kicked back to watch the other teams race around and finalize their antennas, as our (clearly superior) antenna dangled all the way to the ground. Just then, the clueless team appeared to have pulled the winning trick. They had assembled all 200 straws into each other, and they were gradually moving the super long, snakelike straw up the side of a large sand dune. Watching from our Jeep, we realized what was happening. Even though their line was diagonal, their antenna was going to be 50 feet tall! We were stunned silent.

"Guys!" Doron yelled. "We can drive the Jeep up to the top of the sand dune and roll the tail the whole way back down. We can still win!" Within a flash, the eight of us were back to work. Our team leader started to drive the Jeep up the sand dune as we ran after it, racing to connect as many straws as possible in the time we had left. As we approached the top of the dune, a siren went off signaling the end of the exercise.

We were distraught. If the exercise finished ten minutes earlier, we would have won, and if the exercise lasted ten more minutes, we would have had enough time to connect all the straws to the Jeep and we also would have won. Unfortunately, we learned the hard way: our timing was off and everything else was irrelevant.

Time Dictates the Size of Your Map

We tend to think of time as something that either works for or against us. We're familiar with sayings such as, "time is on my side, or "time is working against me." We imagine that as time goes by, we get better, stronger, wiser, or alternatively, slower and less competitive. From the Local Maximum prism, neither can be entirely true, as time is variable.

Just like hiking left can be correct for a while but not indefinitely, so can hiking right. When we were building our straw antenna, time wasn't on our side or against us. We would have won with ten extra minutes or ten less minutes. Our antenna got higher with each step we took, moving from a triangle structure to the Jeep's antenna, and then driving the Jeep up the mountain. We lost because time caught us in a Local Maximum.

The first and most important lesson about time is that it is not linear. It is neither good nor bad, working in my favor or against it. Time is a parameter that has peaks. If you are hiking in a desert looking for the highest peak, your approach will change completely if you have 60 minutes, six hours, or six days, and not because you will do more A/B/X tests or overcome valleys. If the tallest peak is a day's hike away but you only have 60 minutes to get there, it's irrelevant. Time dictates the size of your map of possible outcomes.

This has two important implications. First, if you can change the time, you can change the map. Second, when you can't change the time, any peak outside of the possible outcomes must be disregarded.

For example, imagine you're the head of a business division. You've been given two quarters to bring in $5 million in sales or you'll have to make substantial cuts. Can you persuade your boss to give you four quarters but shift the target to $10 million in sales? Having to show results within a tight time window could push you away from pursuing larger clients that need more time to close. In other words, the larger clients may be a much better strategy, but the only way larger clients can be included on your map of possible outcomes is to increase the time needed to close them. Alternatively, if you will go out of business within two quarters without hitting $5 million in sales, a peak that takes eight months to climb (or, closing larger clients) is irrelevant.

Publicly owned company CEOs often allude to this challenge when they try to explain their decisions to their shareholders during quarterly briefings. The CEOs are trying to steer their companies toward long-term success. However, their investors, who can sell and buy the shares whenever they like, want short-term gains. The CEOs then naturally find themselves in a conundrum. They are willing to move away from short-term Local Maximum routes, but their shareholders and the rest of the stock market may not have the patience to wait.

When asked about taking on big risks that only pay off in the long term, Richard Branson, CEO of the Virgin Group, said, "Fortunately, we are not a public company. We are a private group of companies, and I can do what I want." Branson can chase adventures in space, and given his control, he can change his map, too.

Finding Time and Timing What Matters

The intelligence unit in charge of satellite and high-altitude drones faced a routine challenge. Every week, they received a list of coordinates from a variety of intelligence departments, which required high-resolution aerial photography. To meet these requirements, the unit had a number of unique drones, capable of flying at 30,000 feet to capture the precise images. Officer Naama and two of her soldiers mapped the locations they received, calculated the distances and flight times, and suggested a flight plan for the week that allowed the drones to cover each location three times. The number three was somewhat arbitrary, but common wisdom suggested if the drones took three separate pictures of each location, at the very least, one of them would be clear and free of clouds, birds, or planes.

Once the routes were approved, the team executed their plan by directing the specialized drone pilots and preparing the engineering team to receive the footage dumps at the end of each flight routine. These engineers did their work on the weekends and performed the delicate process of normalizing and then enhancing the footage before returning it back to Naama's team. Then Naama's team filtered out the pictures from the "strips" of data and returned the images to the relevant departments. The entire process was not only complex; it had to comply with the military's strict compliance and clearance policies. Only Naama's team knew all exact locations. The drone pilots only knew their individual locations, the engineers could only see data code lines (but not the pictures), and the final pictures were only seen by the relevant specific departments.

But Naama's team faced a growing problem. Her team's successful execution created an increased demand for more high-resolution pictures. Within a few months, the unit was getting double the coordinate requests that Naama had been receiving when she started her position, and the demand kept increasing.

At first, Naama tried optimizing the routes to cover more coordinates. Then, she clipped the third run; hoping two runs would be enough to get a single clear photo. Before long, with the number of unique drones and pilots capped, three runs were out of the question, two runs was the norm, and in a few extreme cases, some coordinates received only one run. And it didn't take long for the complaints from the different departments to land on her desk, as three runs was really what was needed to ensure one good picture. Everyone was barking demands at her saying, "Do you realize how important this is? I don't care what other departments want! It's crazy that we are being left in the dark at this crucial moment."

Naama and the engineering team tried to figure out how best to optimize their drones and their pilots' limited time. As one engineer put it: at the end of a typical week, 15% of the pictures were useless due to a cloud or obstacle in the way, 55% were good pictures but duplicates (and therefore, not needed), and the remaining 30% were utilized by the requesting departments. The question was how to stop wasting time on unnecessary duplications and how to better use their time to capture the pictures they needed.

After several meetings, brainstorming sessions, and conversations with the general who was overseeing the initiative, they landed on a new plan. Over the course of nine months, they would upgrade the engineering systems so they could be run every evening, as opposed to exclusively on the weekends. The logic was simple: if the engineers could perform their work every evening, Naama could assess the quality of the first-run images and, if they were good, avoid sending the drones back to locations unnecessarily. Basic math suggested this strategy would allow Naama's team to increase their capacity by 250%.

Everyone was excited, especially the engineers as the plan validated the importance of their work, but something about it felt off for Naama. She wasn't an engineer by training and remained quiet during most of the planning discussions. The decision to invest nine months of development to determine the presence of a bird, a cloud, or a plane seemed excessive. Not only would it cost a lot, but she would need two to three times the number of engineers to run the process every night. The weekend photo enhancement process was stressful enough, regardless of how much data they had.

Yes, the new plan optimized their drones and their pilots' time, but there was still a time inefficiency. None of the departments needed the photos daily. All Naama needed to know was whether the photos were good as taken, or if they needed to be enriched by the engineers. Then it clicked. She needed another picture; a really easy one to take that simply showed if the location was obstructed. A standard smartphone camera would do.

Within four weeks, a new solution was implemented. Every evening, one of Naama's junior soldiers received a stack of standard pictures taken by a simple camera on the drone, showing what was below when it reached each coordinate, no development or enrichment required. The soldier ticked a box if the image was clear and made an X if it wasn't. If the picture was clear, Naama knew the enhanced pictures would be clear, and when the box was crossed, they sent the drone out again. This simple fix saved hours of drone and pilot time and eliminated the need to hire extra engineers. We tend to think that the passage of time is inexorable and out of our control. But in fact, there are actions we can take, if not to change the passage of time, then at least to alter the constraining impact it has on us. Naama found time by adding a new step, and that new step launched her team out of the Local Maximum and up a higher mountain.

2030 Goals vs. 2050 Goals

We have a tendency to assume that the milestones along the way to our goals should be measured in similar terms as the final one we are working toward. If I am studying toward my SAT and need to score 1300, I may take a weekly practice exam where starting from 1000, I aim to improve by 50 points each week to peak in 6 weeks' time at my desired score. Similarly, if I am about to launch a new website, I may determine that to reach a million visits, I need to create a strategy to attract 20,000 users each week over the course of a year.

While this type of thinking may work in some cases, in others this step-by-step approach can lead us straight into a Local Maximum Trap. My study strategy may seem solid, but I may have an area of weakness preventing me from reaching my goal that requires me to focus on a few weeks in which I will not see any incremental improvements. Only if I allow myself this downtime to "sharpen my axe" will I stand a chance of achieving my longer-term goal. Similarly, my website strategy for bringing 20,000 new visitors may only work as a one-off and reaching a million through-out the year could require a partnership that only kicks into action in the final three months.

In his book *How to Avoid a Climate Disaster* Bill Gates details why certain policies aimed at making reductions by 2030 may pre-vent humanity from hitting the net-zero emissions target of 2050. "Isn't 2030 a stop on the way to 2050?" he asks, "Not necessarily."

According to Gates, climate policies provide an example of how simply setting a series of increasing goals may lead us to a very problematic Local Maximum. He explains that in order to reach the 2030 goals of reducing emissions, governments may be tempted to replace coal-fired power plants with gas-fired ones. This strategy would clearly reduce emissions over the coming years, but actually likely to be counterproductive in reaching the 2050 net zero goal, would require spending even more money to now dismantle the gas plants. He therefore suggests pursuing strategies that are more likely to lead to success in 2050, even if this means setting aside strategies that might look appealing in the shorter term. Keeping our eye on the real goal of 2050 will help us realize that 2030 is a Local Maximum.

Utilizing Time Limitations

Do you remember the last time you live streamed a sports game? You probably remember how terrible the quality was, especially compared to a YouTube video. Most of us know a live stream is *obviously* going to mean inferior quality, but why is the difference so dramatic? Well, we tell ourselves, because it's live. Why should that matter? Because a live event is much harder to stream and therefore the quality is poorer. But what about watching the game on network TV? The quality isn't poorer there. The inherent difference is related to the way algorithms treat time.

Internet broadband has limited capacity, and this limited capacity isn't always stable. Some milliseconds will be more vacant and allow the transfer of many bytes of data, and other milliseconds will be less so. Watch closely the next time your YouTube video loads. You'll see it does so in chunks, maybe a minute of video at a time, and it always keeps the video a little ahead of where you are. It makes sure that you experience a constant flow of watching, but it doesn't send the information to you constantly, rather every few seconds. When it realizes you are still watching, it loads the next chunk of video. The sensation for the user is that the game is running live, or possibly it was preloaded, but neither are true. YouTube utilizes time to its advantage, and the truth is, very little runs in a smooth and continuous manner.

A live event, on the other hand, can't utilize time in the same manner for a simple reason: they don't know what will happen in a few minutes. They are streaming the event live, whereas YouTube is able to decouple all the moving parts, compress them, send them in bulk, and then run them to the user in a smooth manner; each "chunk" running when it is best suited.

YouTube's process is similar to how Naama solved her unit's coordinate challenge. Taking all those extra photos that were ultimately discarded is like the bytes of live video that reach your computer after the fact. Your computer receives whatever it can and simply projects it onto your screen. It must show a "live event," and often, bytes of data reach it too late, and that data is simply discarded.

Naama's engineers realized that building a system to check the data every evening would eliminate the waste of taking unnecessary duplicate photos. But it would be like YouTube sending each of their users a faster computer to run their videos. Naama further refined the time question when she realized the departments didn't need the photos to be ready at the end of the day. They just needed to be good to go at the end of the week. This mirrors why YouTube doesn't load the entire video in advance; it just needs to ensure each chunk is ready when the user is ready to view it.

We often believe that time limits our potential. And yes, time can be a limiting factor, but making sure those limiting factors are truly necessary can help us to decouple them down to the bare minimum required. Machines and advanced algorithms have learned to perfect this lesson to the millisecond. Just ask any of YouTube's 2.7 billion active users.

Why Now?

In so many aspects of life, timing is crucial. It can make the difference between a huge success and a total failure. Listen to a comedian tell a joke, watch a basketball pro decide when to dribble in for a layup, or notice when a savvy businessman presents his suggestion in a long meeting. You can try the exact same joke, basketball dribble, or business suggestion, but if the timing is wrong, your outcome is likely to be completely different.

There is a time-shape to success. Ask a DJ. He's not going to kick off a party with the biggest hit or the fastest trance beat: that would never work. He's got to play the hit at exactly the right moment when the crowd needs a lift, just as a comedian can't open her set with the joke that is guaranteed to receive the biggest round of applause. Political advisors will tell you they help their candidates build momentum a specific number of months before an election, but not too soon. The same goes for sports teams, who need to be good at the beginning of the season but know they need to hit their ideal stride during the second half of the season.

Mivtza Savta is an old Israeli satirical movie (the name literally translates as Operation Grandma), starring an enthusiastic military officer named Krembo. He famously provided advice on how to succeed in army drills. "I start literally as fast as I can, and then I gradually increase my pace throughout the rest of the course." Unfortunately for Krembo, and many others trying to win a race, carefully pacing yourself from the starting gun through to the final sprint is critical. Push too soon, and you might collapse. Push too late, and you will end with excess energy.

Venture capitalists and start-ups use timing as a strategic tool, too. As the industry has become wiser and learned what to look for early on, the "why now?" slide has become a standard in every start-up presentation. It is not enough to have a great solution, fantastic team, connected partners, or even lots of capital. To succeed, your timing must be right, which is why "why now" has become a staple. This is not to answer, "are we too early or are we too late," but rather why now is the right time to build a business and not hit a plateau. And investors need to understand this as well.

Machine algorithms are constantly taught to ask "why now" is the optimal time, and they have it down to a science: precisely when to advertise on a YouTube clip, how long to run a TikTok video before loading the next one, how often and when to recommend connecting to a Facebook friend, how long before Netflix plays the next episode in a series.

Getting the timing wrong can be catastrophic for innovation. Before there was YouTube, there were earlier iterations that hit the market too soon. Ever heard of ShareYourWorld.com? No one has, but it was the first video hosting site to compress digital data. Later, there was Vimeo and DailyMotion, but these sites missed the "why now" moment.

Innovation is but one example of a path where we attempt to capitalize and maximize on timing decisions. Take the career path. Often, people admit, "I got my dream job too soon" or, "I came into this position too late in my career." Wars have been lost, breakthrough innovations have been wasted, and umpteen millions of opportunities missed as a result of the wrong timing.

No one wants to peak too soon or too late in their job, in a race, in the market, and even in matters of the heart. How many times have you heard a buddy bemoan, "If only I'd met Sara ten years ago, we would be happily married today" or some other such variation? And therein lies the key. Yes, time matters, and yes, timing can be everything, but time is a variable. And variables have optimal points that can be maximized.

The subtitle of this chapter refers to time as "the fourth dimension," which suggests time is a hypothetical construct, and it should be viewed as a mathematical extension of the three-dimensional space we occupy. Through this lens, we can come to accept that time represents possibilities as well as limitations. It is not fixed, it is not linear, and it is not finite.

The implication of time for our ability to navigate our paths is paramount, as time dictates which of the mountains around us are relevant and which, like the new idea of driving the military Jeep to the top of the mountain with our straw antenna, are misleading. Furthermore, learning to break apart the components of time, as both YouTube and Naama demonstrated, can allow us to solve for trade-offs that seem impossible in theory but actually lead us to higher ground. Finally, we learn that the field we are in is not fixed. One mountain could be getting taller while another could be shrinking. Like most ventures, knowing *when* to climb the mountain may be more important than the venture itself.

A Little Byte of Data Science

Every online retailer grapples with the hard choice of trading off accuracy vs. latency. In simple English, it is accurately presenting the items a specific user will most want to buy versus presenting the items quickly. Imagine searching a retailer's website for "Mother's Day Gifts." The site crawls over your data and learns that last year you bought one electronic photo frame out of a set of two. From your online posts, it learns that you and your mother spent a month together in Kenya. And finally, from your cookies, it learns you are planning to visit South America with

(continued)

(continued)

her this summer. The three gift recommendations you receive are highly accurate in terms of what you are likely to buy: the second half of the electronic photo frame set, a miniature Masa Mara Kenyan model of a giraffe (your mom's favorite animal), and a massage coupon for your hotel in South America. Pretty amazing, right? The only problem is the website takes ten minutes to load. Statistically speaking, most users would have left or "clicked away" after three seconds, never mind ten minutes.

Now imagine the opposite problem. At the precise moment you enter "Mother's Day Gifts," you are presented with a webpage populated with kid toys. Not only that, but they don't deliver to your city. The retailer's software developers know that if they give their algorithms more time, they will provide more accurate results, but as time goes on, fewer users will stick around to view them.

If this sounds like a small issue, Walmart estimated that improving their algorithms by only 0.1 seconds would increase their annual revenue by $100 million! Amazon believes this trade-off is even more costly. Their math indicates 0.1 seconds would increase their annual revenue by 1% (much more than 100 million)! Alibaba, eBay, Home Depot, Shopify, Target, and many others have made similar estimates. They are hitting Local Maximums as a result of time. What do the algorithms do to minimize this affect? The three steps we discussed in this chapter:

1. Size of the map: algorithms learn how fast they need to respond to keep users engaged. They are taught this number is not fixed and is therefore flexible. It can increase the amount of time allocated when it is believed the accuracy will dramatically improve. On the other hand, when accuracy isn't improving every few milliseconds, it will

defer to respond faster. This doesn't mean slower responses are more accurate, but rather the algorithms believe they are improving more. (Note: The gaps here are tiny for us humans, but in the machine world, the difference between 0.75 seconds and 0.8 is enormous.)

2. Flexible constraints: retailer websites have learned that half the "answer" is pretty clear from the beginning. Regardless of complex calculations, the website will still choose to present its brand banner, some drop-down options, and space for an advertisement or promotion, which may come later. The space is fixed and accounted for. Therefore, most retail websites load in phases. You may not notice this (it happens very quickly), but next time, watch and pay attention to which parts load first, and which are slightly delayed.

3. Getting the timing right: cutting edge retailers realize there is a path to purchasing. If you decide to buy an electronic photo frame, they have learned when to present the cheap one, the most expensive one, and the one with same-day delivery. Showing a user the very best option straightaway is not always optimal for them, but taking their users down a path with a successful outcome has proven to be wiser.

Chapter 7

Global Maximum Equilibrium vs. Self-Interest

Alone we can do so little; together we can do so much.

– Helen Keller

O n the third day of the weeklong tryouts for Special Forces, there is a landmark drill that officers use to identify some of the key characteristics required for the unit. The sandbag drill takes place (surprise!) in the desert. It starts with the cadets standing in a circle facing each other, roughly a dozen of them, each a few feet away from each other. In the center, there is a pile of empty 20-kilo sandbags. The drill lasts 60 minutes, at the end of which they will receive a group score equal to the number of filled sandbags at the center of their circle. They will also receive a personal score calculated as follows: one point for every sandbag in the center plus two points for each individual sandbag placed next to them.

The point of the drill is to assess how individuals work within teams. Those who are physically stronger and mentally more determined will naturally collect more sandbags than they can distribute. However, each cadet has to decide every time they finish filling a sandbag: Does it go in the group pile in the center or in their individual pile?

Watching the exercise is extremely telling, especially because the drill is typically performed several times consecutively. At first, a cadet might rush to collect as many individual sandbags as he can. But as the drill is performed numerous times, gradually the rules allow cadets to collaborate with a few of their peers and they form groups: the collaborators and the individuals. Interestingly, the collaborators not only score higher as a result of their collaboration, but they also tend to work harder as the pressure mounts to justify their place within the group. The soldiers who opt for the individual approach by piling sandbags next to their own spots choose a path that ultimately limits their potential.

If you were to run the sandbag exercise with 10 cadets, and 6 of them work together to pool all of their sandbags in the center of their circle while the other four work individually, there is no doubt the group will work better. The challenge for the group is to stay unified without anyone breaking away to place a few sandbags in their personal pile toward the end of the drill. Often, though not always, one of the stronger cadets will do this and that is when the group starts falling apart. Their success relies on the *belief* that the group approach will hold together.

The individual approach is more limiting than the group approach. If a group of 10 cadets collects 10 sandbags each during the drill, they will all score 20 points; two for each sandbag that lies in their individual piles. If any of them moves a sandbag to the middle, they will only score 19 points, but it doesn't make sense for them to do so. At 20 points each, they are at an Individual Maximum.

This drill is an interesting test of character. Do you view yourself as an individual, with all bags near you at your maximum, or as part of a group, with your bags in the center? Do you change your approach based on how other people act? For example, if someone else starts working individually, do you feel like a sucker putting your bags in the middle or do you continue to do so? And finally, do you try and persuade others to put their bags in the middle when you are simply taking sandbags to your own pile?

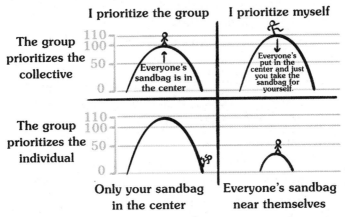

All of the sandbags in the center is a Group Maximum, whereas all the sandbags next to each cadet is an Individual Maximum. Every time a cadet moves a sandbag to the center, he is moving up the group mountain, but he is heading down the individual mountain. The opposite is also true. Every time a cadet moves a sandbag to his own pile, he is moving up the individual mountain but down the collective mountain.

The exercise demonstrates not only how good you are at filling up sandbags, but to what extent you view yourself as an individual or part of the collective.

Optimizing for the Group

In a 1993 study, British anthropologist Robin Dunbar searched for cognitive clues to determine the optimal group size. Remarkably, after researching a variety of different animals, he found a correlation between proportionate size of the brain's neocortex to the size of social groups in primates. For instance, Tamarin monkeys, with a brain size ratio of approximately 2.3, typically have social groups of around 5 members. In contrast, Macaque monkeys, with a larger brain size ratio of 3.8, are often found in much bigger groups, averaging about 40 members. According to these findings, Dunbar's "social brain hypothesis" theorized that humans are ideally suited for social groups of approximately 150 individuals, a size he equated to a "clan."[1]

In his 2000 book, *The Tipping Point*, Malcolm Gladwell explored the concept of the "Dunbar Number" in depth.[2] He illustrated the power of keeping human groups below 150 using the example of W. L. Gore and Associates, the company behind Gore-Tex. The firm's leadership found through experimentation that when over 150 employees were housed in a single building, various social issues arose. To address this, they began constructing facilities designed for no more than 150 workers, complete with an equal number of parking spaces. Once these spaces were occupied, the company would erect another building for an additional 150 employees. True to the Dunbar Number, keeping offices below 150 people increased performance.

The Dunbar Number has only gained in popularity since. Some have suggested the reason for the military's success in keeping companies between the range of 100 to 200 soldiers can be attributed to Dunbar's theory. Amongst others, in 2007, the Swedish Tax Agency dictated a maximum of 150 employees per office, referring to Dunbar's research.

Similar to the sandbag exercise, society often faces situations where it must decide if working together to prioritize the group provides a greater benefit than prioritizing our own needs individually. On the one hand, a larger group allows us to benefit from more of each other, but on the other hand, as the group grows, we lose our sense of inclusiveness and end up acting individually when working together as a group becomes harder.

As humans have grouped together more over the centuries, living not just in groups of tens and hundreds, but thousands and millions, we have added laws, social contracts, and expected norms in an attempt to continue prioritizing the group, even though we are a smaller part of it. A simple example is the law against littering in the streets. As an individual, I may prefer to simply throw an empty can of soda out the window as I drive down an empty highway. But if everyone chucked their soda cans out the window, I would be living in a neighborhood full of trash, and driving down the street may even be dangerous due to the abundance of litter. This social norm ensures we prioritize the group so we, as individuals, all benefit from a clean community.

Darwin's Warning: The Kevins Among Us

Charles Darwin's evolutionary theory of natural selection did not, unfortunately, predict the survival of the fairest or the altruistic. If a clan of 20 cavemen ran low on food, they'd have a better chance of survival if they band together to scour for supplies. Not to mention, they could protect each other from external enemies who might try to take the little food they do have. However, there is usually at least one person in every group, let's call him Kevin, who sneaks a few bites of food without others noticing. And Kevin, by behaving selfishly, is better positioned to survive. Hence, Darwin's theory suggests our ancestors, the ones that didn't starve, were cooperative but selfish individuals.

Naturally, a society made up of Kevins will hit a Local Maximum. A group of Kevins running the sandbag exercise will agree to work together. They will put bags in the center to encourage everyone else to do so, too. But at the very end of the exercise, the Kevins will keep the last sandbag or two for themselves. The extreme Kevin will also conserve energy during the first three quarters of the exercise. And when he switches gears to focus on himself, he still has gas left in the tank to increase his own sandbagging output and score more total points. Watching the military drills, one can see that certain groups do turn into Kevins. One guy starts off doing something he thinks is smart, but before long, they are all acting selfishly and losing points as a result. Once a group of Kevins forms, it is very hard to snap out of the Local Maximum they are in.

Darwin wasn't the only one to predict this is where humanity might get stuck. The British philosopher and evolutionary biologist Richard Dawkins also suggested as much in his book *The Selfish*

Gene when he said, "Let us understand what our own selfish genes are up to, because we may then at least have the chance to upset their designs."[3]

Our genes are geared toward Dunbar's magic number of 150, but other forces, such as technology and sociology, are grouping us together in larger and larger numbers. This raises challenges, as we are typically able to score well in a sandbag exercise and limit our "Keviness" so long as the groups are small, but when they get big, I mean very big, things get much harder. Maybe we can learn from creatures with different genes and different ego designs?

Learn from the Ant

At the heart of the Group vs. Individual debate lies our ego. Research on the influence of ego on group dynamics shows that high levels of egocentrism lead to bad outcomes for groups, as it reduces the collective responsibility for the group's performance.[4] A stronger ego results in a more individual approach with less responsibility toward the group (this is what the military is testing for with the sandbags). The size of the group matters, too: the larger the group, the more it takes for us to care about it. Other studies have shown that the size of the group affects how selfishly we will act, because larger groups make us feel smaller and less connected to others.[5] Therefore, it takes more pressure for us to act generously.

Numerous studies have been devoted to the question as to whether insects have egos. While the research points in different directions, ants seem to be quite extreme in the collective approach. When a food source has been located, they will release chemicals as a signal to the rest of the colony to come and help carry the food back to the nest. And when the nest is attacked, ants behave in a remarkable way, sacrificing themselves – sometimes hundreds or even thousands in number – to save the queen and allow the colony to survive.[6,7] Behaviorally, when scientists dropped a spoonful of ants into a cup of water, the ants didn't devolve into a panicked, every-man-for-himself frenzy that we might expect from humans.

(Drowning often happens in pairs when a panicked victim drags a would-be rescuer down.) Rather, the ants were observed quickly forming themselves into a sort of raft to increase the total buoyancy of the group and their collective chance of survival.

It's no surprise ants have survived for millions of years; they don't have Kevins. They can avoid the pull of individual ego thinking that leads to Local Maximums and act as a cohesive group. (Interestingly, insects' brains are wired differently and don't have a neocortex.) If the ants were running the sandbag exercise, even if the group was enormous, all the sandbags would end up in the center. In fact, you can literally watch a group of ants at work and witness their collective work ethic in practice. A colony of ants will exceed Dunbar's Number by hundreds of thousands, and still work together harmoniously, prioritizing the group's needs over their own. It's hard to imagine that hundreds of thousands of ants know each other personally and care about one another, but they certainly act as though they do. Critically, ants are unburdened by the human limitation of the ego, which traps us in Individual Maximums. And though the Kevins survived evolution, a society of Kevins is a surefire formula to quickly hit a Group Maximum.

We Approach, but with Caution

A well-known parable seems to have been first told by a roaming 19th-century preacher, Rabbi Haim of Romshishok. He began his talks with the following story:

> *"One night, I ascended to the heavens. I was first taken to see Hell and the sight was horrifying. Row after row of tables were loaded with dishes of magnificent food, yet the people seated around the tables were thin and pale, all crying of hunger. As I took a closer look, I understood their difficulty. Each person's arms were tied with wooden boards so he could not bend either elbow to bring the food to his mouth. It broke my heart to see these poor people tortured as they held their food but couldn't eat it.*

> *Next, I was taken to visit Heaven. I was shocked to see the same setting I had witnessed in Hell: the tables, the food, and even the wooden boards around their elbows. But unlike in Hell, the people in Heaven were enjoying themselves, laughing and relaxed. As I took a closer look, I watched a man pick up his spoon, dig it into the dish before him and feed his neighbor. His neighbor thanked him and returned the favor with a smile.*"[8]

The "we" approach has many advantages, especially as it allows us to climb toward higher ground that can't be achieved individually. However, it must be noted, it is often individualism that acts as the scout and finds higher grounds. It was Marie Curie's and Steve Jobs's audacity to go against mainstream beliefs that led to groundbreaking inventions, Rosa Parks' and Malala Yousafzai's bravery that elevated women's voices, and it was thanks to Raoul Wallenberg's and Oskar Schindler's moral courage during World War II that thousands of Jews were saved.

On the one hand, we often reach a point where we are only able to continue moving upwards if we work as a collective. On the other hand, the individual often acts as an X, wandering around, innovating, questioning, and championing new ideas. It is he who finds the mountains we wouldn't have found as a group. Therefore, it's not surprising that socialistic or collective approaches perform well in the short term, as societies climb up and people can lean on one another for support. However, eventually, as societies tend to clamp down on individual rights, they fall behind in the long run when X thinking is discouraged.

A successful, long-term formula is one that allows for these two values to coincide. Individual freedom encourages diverse perspectives, leading to creativity and innovation, while social bonds and relationships increase a sense of community and collaboration. As Bob Dylan said, "I think of a hero as someone who understands the degree of responsibility that comes with his freedom."

This Is Not a Joke: A Cinematic Prisoner's Dilemma

The climactic scene in Christopher Nolan's *Batman: The Dark Knight* (2008),[9] the second film in the trilogy, features two enormous ferryboats. One carries ordinary civilians and the other carries prisoners escorted by police. Both boats suddenly lose communication, the lights flicker, and to everyone's horror, they discover that the hull of each of boat has been loaded with TNT. Suddenly, the power partially returns and the passengers on both boats hear the evil Joker's voice crackle over the ships' megaphones:

> *"Tonight, you are all going to be a part of a social experiment. I am ready to blow you all sky high. Anyone attempts to get off their boat, you all die. Each of you has a remote. . .to blow up the other boat. At midnight, I blow you all up. If, however, one of you presses the button, I'll let that boat live. So, who's it going to be: you or the Batman? Decide! Or give me your remotes and let me do it."*

With an hour until midnight, the dilemma is clear. Each boat can wait and not press the button. As long as the other boat does the same, they will survive. This is an equilibrium: they can continue to survive this way for an hour. But it is a weak equilibrium, as every moment, there's a chance the other boat will press the button. It is in each boat's interest to press the button a second before the other boat does. The evil Joker's added twist of threatening to kill them all at midnight adds to the weight of the decision.

Do you press the button one second before midnight? Maybe the other boat realizes this threat and decides to press the button two seconds before midnight? This logic suggests another solution, though not an optimal one, and that is for each boat to simply press their button as soon as possible.

The scene intensifies as arguments break out on both boats. A civilian woman cries out, "The other boat is full of prisoners. They had their chance!" At one point, the civilian boat attempts to tally a vote to determine what they should do. As midnight draws near and tension increases, there is a powerful moment when both boats appreciate they are only alive because the other boat hasn't pressed their button. They don't know each other, but suddenly there is a clear bond between them, even a level of trust.

On the prisoner's boat, a particularly large and mean looking man gets up, slowly walks over to the officer holding the detonator, and says in a low voice, "You don't want to die, but you don't know how to take a life. Give it to me." After a long pause, he continues, "You can tell them I took it by force. Give it to me, and I'll do what you should have done 10 minutes ago." With one minute to midnight, the officer gives the large prisoner the detonator who instantly throws it overboard (becoming a hero, as no one can now press that detonator).

Simultaneously, the tally is counted on the civilian boat with a majority in favor of pressing the button. But who will press it? A middle-aged man, who had been persuading others to vote in favor of pressing the button, suddenly says, "Nobody wants to get their hands dirty. I'll do it." He walks slowly to the detonator, but he can't bring himself to press the button.

Midnight strikes and both boats are still intact.

The Joker's cold calculation was not wrong. He was banking on the weakness of the equilibrium, and figured, eventually, one boat would think selfishly of themselves first and press the button. After which, there is no turning back. But no one does press the button. When pushed into a moral dilemma of epic proportions, the people opt for the collective good over self-interest.

Yes, *Batman: The Dark Knight* is a movie, and actually quite a good one. It is a cinematic Prisoner's Dilemma in that it emphasizes the natural conflict and challenge of balancing personal gain against the potential for mutual benefit. But we see this type of behavior in numerous social interactions, even in small everyday interactions.

Imagine the driver of a car realizing he needs to switch lanes at a red light. It's not in the other car's interest to let the driver cut in when the light turns green, but our values or social norms push us to do so, and even more so, if we make a connection through a quick glance at each other. Here too, there are two equilibriums: a Global Maximum where we help one another and are therefore better off, and a Local Maximum where we are all selfish and act in line with our own needs. But eventually, we all will pay the price for acting this way, and one day, we will be the one in the car who needs to cut into a lane.

Other examples include the arms race between nations, over-fishing in shared waters, price wars in oligopolistic markets, trade wars, and environmental pollution, to name a few. In each of these examples, we see individuals, businesses, and nations grapple with the trade-off between cooperation and self-interest. The challenge is that the Local Maximum self-interest path is typically a strong equilibrium, meaning no one can improve their outcome by them-selves, whereas the Global Maximum cooperative equilibrium is weak; each individual can improve his or her position by acting selfishly, but we will then slide down to the selfish Local Maximum point. Can we steer toward our Global Cooperative Maximum?

It turns out that the principal factors dictating the altitude we can reach, more even than our stamina or skill, are our social norms and shared values. A family, sports team, company, or nation can reach a better outcome as long as its shared values and norms enable it to maintain its Global Maximum Equilibrium. If these beliefs break down, so does our potential.

A Little Byte of Data Science

There are huge implications for whether we act as individuals or as part of a group. In the early days of computers, engineers had to teach the algorithms how to behave: Push ahead of your neighbor or let your neighbor go first? Do you program your computer's software to run FIFO or LIFO?

(continued)

(continued)

According to FIFO (First In First Out), the software should execute tasks in the order in which they are given. There are many arguments in favor of this approach. One is that it is simpler. If I want the computer to perform task 1, then task 2, and then task 3, that is naturally the way I will provide it the instructions (not 3, then 2, and finally 1).

According to LIFO (Last In First Out), the software should start by executing the most recent task and work backwards. Here too, there are numerous advantages. One being that LIFO is typically advantageous in memory management, as the last item added to the stack is the first one to be removed.

The FIFO vs. LIFO debate is an optimization challenge. Your smartphone software scans down the list of tasks it needs to prioritize: downloading the next three seconds of the Instagram video you are watching so it doesn't buffer, alerting you to the receipt of a WhatsApp message, or having your calendar notify you of a meeting in 10 minutes' time. (Truth be told, your smartphone is juggling many more tasks than these at any point in time.) Which task goes first?

Historically, computer scientists debated these approaches and tested to find which situations favored FIFO vs. LIFO. However, with time, it became increasingly clear that neither were optimal. In both scenarios, the tasks were acting "selfishly." Whichever task's turn it was to be performed didn't make room for anyone else and held up the entire line until its task was done. In other words, the tasks were a single lane of cars in traffic. No one allowed anyone else in, and the debate switched focus to whether we should try and clear the traffic jam from the front (FIFO) or the back (LIFO).

While FIFO and LIFO are still taught in Computing 101, the main question engineers are working on today is how to look at the whole task list. The goal is to find an optimal solution for the entire system instead of the individual tasks.

When doing so, engineers find solutions for the traffic jam equivalent to the following:

1. Some cars won't continue the whole way straight through the traffic jam. Some will turn right, where there is no traffic at all, and we can open a lane early to allow all the cars turning right to skip through.
2. When the traffic light at the end of the congestion turns yellow before it turns red, quickly squeeze any fast cars or motorbikes through before traffic stops again.
3. If a car has a flat tire, allow for a side-lane to park the problematic car while it gets fixed, rather than make the whole line of cars wait for the tire to be fixed.
4. If an ambulance, police car, or fire engine comes through with a siren, all other cars will move aside to allow the emergency vehicle through quickly.
5. In recent years, data scientists have been focusing on how to allow multiple drivers to pool together, thereby reducing the number of cars on the road. The remaining cars are able to travel in a more cooperative manner when there is less traffic.

Chapter 8

Dangerous Mountains

Mountains pose a constant challenge. Even the most experienced climbers know they can never conquer them; they can only hope to negotiate their passage.

— Jon Krakauer

Let's revisit our paratrooper scenario from Chapter 1. You're back out in the Negev Desert, attempting to climb to the top of the highest mountain. You have familiarized yourself with the map; you've sent out scouts to assess the terrain; and you have taken every measure possible to travel across the deep valleys, while staying agile and optimizing your routes within the allotted time. Even if you can clearly see the highest mountain peak (your Global Maximum), and you can also clearly see the shortest direct path to get there, which might be the only path, there are still certain practicalities that might prohibit you from taking it. Why? Because the shape of the mountain is simply too dangerous. The conditions that make certain mountain shapes dangerous need to be taken into consideration.

Just like navigating mountains in the desert, there are many situations in the real world where a route is too perilous to traverse, even though it could lead to a fantastic outcome. In this chapter, I have highlighted the four common dangerous mountain shapes to be wary of when navigating our own paths. Computers have learned to flag each of these shapes as problematic and therefore they must be programmed/navigated with extreme caution if not avoided altogether. Humans, take note, for these same shapes appear in our lives more frequently than we might think. We can apply the same cautionary measures computer algorithms have learned to apply to reduce our proclivity for such shapes.

Uneven Terrain: Volatility

We often find ourselves excelling in career paths, building businesses according to our roadmaps, or thriving in our personal relationships only to discover those paths can take sudden and destabilizing turns. As you've no doubt experienced, some paths are smooth and uneventful while others are rough and uneven.

Not all mountains allow for a smooth ascent. Therefore, aside from choosing the tallest mountain, we need to make sure we are able to overcome the volatility, meaning the ups and downs, along the way.

For example, a start-up centered on a singular event, such as a breakthrough in the development of a new drug, is prone to high volatility in comparison to a business built on continuous successes, such as opening a burger franchise. Similarly, a career as a professional athlete is far less predictable than a more stable career path, such as accounting. It is true an accountant may suddenly get promoted or fired, but the projected path is more predictable than that of the athlete, who could suffer an irreversible injury and have no choice but to change careers. Alternatively, he could win a big game and become a branded name, catapulting him to stardom, sponsorships, and global notoriety. But even when athletes are at the very top of their game, a penalty, a missed shot, or moment of rage can redefine their entire career.

Regardless of the starting point or the potential maximum, we often don't question whether our tolerance for stability and sustainability suits the path we chose. We choose, instead, to focus on the height of the mountain. The mountaineer might be able to gain 800 meters on an ascent, roll back down 450 meters, and then climb another 600, but how long can he sustain such volatility? How long can he endure the uneven terrain?

The mountaineer is not the only person who needs to consider such factors. Let's compare three different types of money managers seeking investors: a CEO of a well-established public company who tries to persuade the public to buy his stock, a hedge fund manager who collects money from investors to invest in a collection of diversified stocks, and a venture capital firm that invests in early-stage, high-risk start-ups. All three managers have the same goal – to make their investors as much money as possible – and all three strategies can lead to potentially very good outcomes. However, the volatility they are each able to endure differs dramatically.

A public company stock is subject to daily trading, and the CEO is keenly aware of the position this puts him in. While he may have numerous valid ideas for continued growth, he must constantly provide his investors with a reason to buy his stock now, and he must convince those who own his stock, not to sell. The pressure to consistently perform, and to perform well, can prohibit the CEO from executing on his grander ideas. In fact, some public companies are under so much pressure to perform, they might not be willing to risk even six months of poor performance in exchange for a huge payout down the road. So, even though the public company's goal is to create long-term value for its investors, it often cannot withstand even a single quarter of downturn. What if a Genie were to appear and tell the CEO his company can be wildly successful if only he is willing to endure three years of terrible performance? Most public CEOs are unlikely to accept such a rocky road. Let's say Apple stock plummets by 80%, and Tim Cook has a foolproof plan to quadruple stock value in two years. Despite the company's track record, he's probably not willing (or able) to take the hit. The investors are unlikely to stick around when they can sell so easily and buy stock in a better-performing company. They may not admit it, but they want a smooth and steady, predictable, reliable road.

A hedge fund manager, who invests in stocks for his clients, is also expected to create long-term value for his investors. While his investors can leave the fund whenever they want in theory, there is typically some degree of stickiness. The investors either have to pay a small fee to leave, provide a few months' notice, or fulfill some other type of preventative measure that gives the hedge fund some security regarding its investor base. The magical genie approaching a hedge fund manager with a tempting scenario will certainly find a greater appetite for his offer from a hedge fund manager than he will from the CEO of a publicly traded company. "Maybe not three years of terrible performance," says the hedge fund manager, "but one or two years is totally doable."

Finally, let's consider the uneven terrain a venture capital (VC) investor is able to endure. A VC firm has a huge advantage over the other two types of money managers in that its investors are legally bound to stay for the entire period of investment (which can sometimes exceed 10 years!), whether they like it or not. The investors are committed, and the funding is secure. This means the VC investor can tolerate ups and downs. They can scout for start-ups that may not generate value in the next 24 hours, or even the next 24 months, but that stand the chance of generating huge profits over longer periods of time. (Despite running a VC firm, I'm not necessarily pitching VC investment. I'm simply pointing out a VC's advantage in this specific regard.) The genie's magical offer is music to the VC firm's ears; they can easily take bigger risks, traverse uneven terrain, and tolerate volatility.

These differences can be found in all types of innovation, career progression, sports scoring methods, and many other aspects of our lives. Politicians, for example, must assess how much negativity they can endure in the press and for how long. Even if they're on a path to the top, there is a limit to how many blows they can withstand (similar to professional athletes). Of course, everyone wants a nice smooth path, but your personality, your business, and/or your long-term goals will determine how well you can navigate an uneven route. Whatever the environment or initiative, before choosing to climb, assess how resilient you are to volatility, and remember, it's often the journey, not the destination, that can make all the difference.

The Single Ascent: No Way Down

In 2004, at the age of 20, Elizabeth Holmes dropped out of Stanford's School of Engineering to "democratize healthcare" with her newborn company, Theranos. The company was founded a year earlier, and with the full backing of her advisor and Stanford's Engineering Dean, Elizabeth was emboldened to ditch her education and devote herself to entrepreneurship. Under her guidance as CEO, Theranos developed a proprietary device named the Edison machine, intended to conduct a wide array of sophisticated blood testing, in virtually any environment, at a significantly lower cost and in a less invasive manner than any other device of its kind on the market. All Edison required to run hundreds of tests on a patient was a few drops of blood.

Theranos and Holmes quickly caught the attention of numerous, high-profile wealthy investors – Rupert Murdoch and Larry Ellison famously among them – who poured money into her vision.

They helped cultivate Elizabeth's reputation and image as the "Next Steve Jobs." Elizabeth was so enamored of Apple's founder that she dressed like him, favoring a wardrobe of black turtlenecks to further fuel the comparisons. By 2014, at the age of 30, she had been featured on the covers of *Fortune*, *Forbes*, and *Inc.* magazines, was named the world's youngest self-made female billionaire (worth $4.5B), ranked #110 on the Forbes 400 List, and had grown her company's valuation to $9 billion.

In 2013, Theranos partnered with Walgreens for $140 million to make the Edison available across 40 locations in California and Arizona. Not long after, the company signed a $367 million contract with Safeway, a large US grocery and pharmacy chain. Holmes's media exposure and Theranos's high-profiled national partnerships led to deeper scrutiny in the validity of the company's promises, and Holmes would have been wise to have had a backup plan. But that was not in her nature. In a 2019 documentary about her meteoric ascent called *The Inventor*, director Alex Gibney, said: "Elizabeth Holmes wanted it all, and she was prepared to do whatever it took to get it."[1] And she herself is quoted as saying: "The minute you have a backup plan, you've admitted you're not going to succeed."[2]

Rumors started to circulate that the Edison wasn't as reliable as Theranos claimed it to be. An investigative *Wall Street Journal* article in 2015[3] questioned whether the technology was any more accurate than the current solutions in use, and executives at Safeway grew concerned when Theranos failed to deliver after raising over $900 million. Before long, Theranos, Elizabeth Holmes, and the Edison machine came crashing down in a spectacular sequence of events as it became clear that without any way of descending the mountain she had climbed, Holmes had been lying to her employees and defrauding investors.

The Centers for Medicare and Medicaid Services (CMS) imposed sanctions on Theranos and revoked certifications for its Newark, California, laboratory. Soon after, Walgreens terminated its partnership with the company. And in 2016, Theranos encountered a series of lawsuits from investors, patients, and numerous regulating bodies. Amid the backlash, the distrust, and the disarray, the company dissolved in 2018 as Elizabeth faced federal charges of fraud and conspiracy to commit wire fraud. After a widely publicized 11-week trial involving 29 witnesses, Elizabeth Holmes was sentenced to 11 years and 3 months in a Texas prison on Friday, November 18, 2022.

It's worth stating the obvious: any mountain that involves fraud is a dangerous mountain. During her trial, Elizabeth said she never meant to build a get rich scheme; she genuinely wanted to help humanity and democratize healthcare. She claims numerous scientists told her the technology either worked, could work, or was nearly on the brink of working. She saw a clear a path to success that nothing and no one could prevent her from traveling. But her path was extremely narrow and became even narrower as she climbed.

Sometimes, a narrow single ascent can lead to success, but not this time. In Holmes's case, her narrow single ascent left her no way to get down off the dangerous mountain she had staked her future upon. The path was closed, there was no room to turn around, no guardrails, and without a backup plan, she fell very hard.

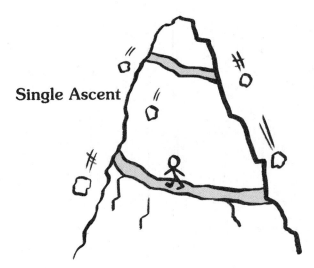

Occasionally, we should avoid a good mountain as the path up is singular and therefore doesn't offer any room to maneuver or pivot.

The "Impossible" Summit: Steepest Peaks

Imagine you're back in the Negev Desert, still looking for the highest peak. You see a magnificent mountain to the Northeast and surely, it's the one. Before setting out, you take a pair of binoculars out of your backpack and spend a few minutes scouting the terrain and planning your route. Overall, you are pleased with your findings and believe you can reach the peak in the allotted time. The mountain is assuredly the tallest in the range, and most of the climb offers a friendly, manageable path. However, the final ascent might be impossible. A few more minutes of studying the terrain reveals a frustrating reality: there is no navigable way to the very top. It might as well be K2, deadlier than Everest, and steeper than the Matterhorn. Yes, you're pretty sure you can ascend 90% of it, but the last 10% may be impossible. Do you attempt the climb?

A nice mountain but followed by a nearly impossible final climb.

This question, or shall I say, this type of terrain, is more common than we might believe. It shows up in any scenario or endeavor where being "good" is easily achievable. Being "very good" is also doable, but being excellent, or even the very best, can take years and years. And even then, success is not guaranteed.

Let's say you want to improve your tennis game. With a few one-on-one lessons, you are likely to see dramatic improvements straightaway. You might start winning matches and join a league. You might even become ranked. But gradually, each incremental gain becomes increasingly difficult. The ascent from being a ranked player to center court at Wimbledon is a nearly impossible journey. We can't all be Novak Djokovic, and GOAT status is a rare achievement.

The same practicality applies across a wide array of examples. When learning to play the guitar, with just a few chords, you can play thousands of songs fairly quickly. But becoming a true Jimi Hendrix–level master requires years of ongoing dedication, and possibly not even then. Engineers constantly face this, especially when dealing with artificial intelligence capabilities. A program can provide swift and amazing results but breaking through a critical accuracy barrier can demand millions of work hours. A pharmaceutical scientist may invent a new drug that is effective for a select number of cancer patients but landing on the cure is a peak yet to be summited. We have developed treatments, yes, but a cure, no. We have seen infrastructure projects reach 90% effectiveness with fairly straightforward efforts. Think of the delivery of electricity, broadband cable, and clean water. Reaching 90% of society is doable, but getting to those final few percentages, who live in distant villages, is very challenging. Similarly, delivery companies such as Amazon or FedEx move parcels from one continent to another fairly cheaply, but the last mile to your doorstep incurs the most cost/pain. Overcoming the last 5% or climbing the last few meters on the King of Mountains is not simply a matter of taking another few steps. The final gasp is the hardest hurdle to overcome.

A key question when examining this terrain, and the steepest peak, is: How crucial is reaching the very top to succeed? In what cases is being "very good" or achieving 95% enough?

We see this in career decisions. As parents, we may prefer our children choose to become lawyers or doctors, rather than football players or pop stars. A decent lawyer or doctor is a respectable and satisfying career path, and the shapes of these paths don't require reaching the very top to be successful. However, only 1.6% of college NCAA players ever make it to the NBA. The statistics for becoming a successful pop star are even slimmer.

Getting to 100% is not always a requirement, while other times, not getting to 100% can be a deal breaker. Imagine a business class airline seat that only reclines 95%. Yes, that may deter a few of the more demanding clientele but not most. On the other hand, how likely is it to matter if a plane is deemed to be only 95% safe?

Don't misunderstand. We should aim high. And sometimes, certain goals require huge risks. But we should make sure we are aware of the risk before setting off to climb the mountain. Does our mountain require us reaching the very top, and how hard is that final climb? Too often, the mountain looks attractive from afar but becomes increasingly harder to climb the closer you get to the top. As Paul Simon wrote, "You know the nearer your destination, the more you're slip slidin' away."

It's important to know before you go if the peak is borderline insurmountable. Building this awareness into decision-making is critical in computer programming these days, and we want to avoid slip sliding away off of an impossible summit.

Higher Ground and Lower Ground

Commonly, we tend to focus on ensuring we make the right decisions every step of the way without checking that we are broadly heading in the right direction. I refer to this tendency as low grounds and high grounds, which is nicely illustrated in the decision tree diagram.

At each point, you need to choose left vs. right with the goal of getting to the highest number. The right side is clearly "high ground." But if we choose each branch individually, rather than assessing the "highest points on the whole," we'll find ourselves in low ground territory at a Local Maximum on the left.

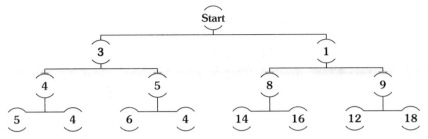

If you choose every branch individually, going left from the start at 3 points, you will naturally choose right at the next juncture (5 points) and finally choose left at the bottom (6 points). If, however, you broaden your perspective, you will realize your general direction should be toward the right side (even without navigating all the way to the far right, at 18 points).

In a hedge fund, the fund manager will dictate the macro-outlook. This determines which sectors the fund will be "long" in (investing in) and which sectors will be "short" (selling). This outlook then affects all the sector analysts. So, for example, if the fund is going to be "long" on airlines, the relevant analysts will analyze the airline stocks and try to determine which will perform best. If, on the other hand, the fund manager determines the fund will go "short" on airlines, the analysts will concentrate their research on building a case for which airlines will perform the worst.

Thus, there are two key elements to building a hedge fund portfolio. The first is the macro-outlook (high ground) to determine which sectors you do and do not want to have stocks in. The second is the micro action of stock picking (low ground) within each sector to determine which specific stocks you want to buy or sell. Which is more important to get right?

Nearly always, the macro sector outlook is dramatically more impactful than the micro stock selection. A sentiment commonly expressed by many investors and analysts in the field of macro investing states that successful investing is about identifying major economic trends and investing in sectors that align with those trends. Stocks are just the vehicles through which these trends play out.

American Airlines may outperform United or Alaska Airlines, but it's not often they will perform dramatically differently. Most of the challenges and growth opportunities within any given sector, be it airline or big tech, are similar. The management teams are learning from each other, and individual companies within a sector typically move up or down at similar paces.

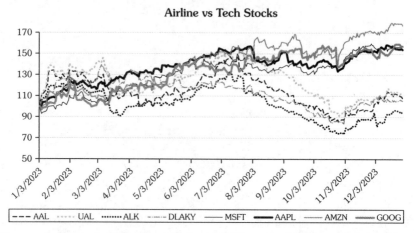

Airline vs Tech Stocks

The graph shows how stocks within a specific sector often move in tandem. Picking which sector to invest in carries more weight than picking the individual stock within the sector.

Anyone who invested in tech stocks 10 to 15 years ago probably did very well. Now, if you invested in Apple instead of Facebook, you might have a done a little better, but you still did well. You landed on high ground with your tech stock investment. Tech was the place to be. But if you invested in airlines – be it EasyJet, Southwest, or American – you probably did poorly.

The idea of there being a "high ground" and a "low ground" is not unique to stocks. This concept applies to situations where one group represents a "winning bucket" whereas another group is more likely to produce losers. Sometimes, being part of the *right* group is more important than being the *best* of the group. Many of the world's greatest discoveries have been made as a consequence of being in the right group of creators, innovators, disruptors, artists, scientists, engineers, etc. Breakthroughs tend to happen in bursts and often transpire within similar time periods and comparable eras.

As mentioned in previous chapters, when your navigation app is tasked with calculating "the fastest route," there are simply too many options to try them all, whether it's Waze, Google Maps, or Apple Maps. One strategy these software algorithms use is to ask: Where is the group of good results? A good group may be one that chooses the highway or one that avoids congested areas, construction, or accidents. In other words, when faced with a difficult challenge, rather than try to land on the perfect answer, the algorithm focuses on reaching the "high ground."

Often, it is more important to be amongst the "high ground" even if you're not at the top, than at the top of the "low ground."

The key to successfully navigating any mountain – your career, your investment portfolio, your start-up idea, or simply getting from A to Z – is to recognize that the shape of the mountain is often more important, and can pose greater challenges, than the height of the mountain alone. Uneven terrain, a single ascent path, the "impossible" final push to the summit, and high ground vs. low ground are all factors to consider to avoid getting stuck in a limiting Local Maximum. Dangerous mountain shapes and their inherent specific conditions will predetermine the success or failure of your initiative.

A Little Byte of Data Science

As algorithms, either directly or indirectly, are increasingly making more decisions in our lives, the engineers programing them are taught to guide them away from dangerous mountains. These mountains may look good and may do well in many scenarios, but they could also lead to disastrous failures. Algorithms, like humans, can predict when they are heading toward a dangerous mountain, and try to choose a different route to avoid an unsafe outcome.

For example, when search engines such as Google are queried for problematic topics, the algorithm gets nervous about providing a certain set of results, even though they are most likely to be the correct ones. The primary example of this is pornography, which Google will attempt to steer away from. Unless the site or query is written explicitly, it will avoid such answers. In other words, even though that path may seem better, because of the danger in getting it wrong, the algorithm steers away.

Another example is when applications involve the use of personal data, location tracking, or facial recognition. An algorithm may intentionally reduce its capabilities to protect the privacy of individuals. Similarly, there are many scenarios such as hiring, insurance policies, and mortgage approvals where pushing algorithms toward perfect accuracy may exacerbate discrimination.

In these examples, there is an inherent risk of the algorithms getting too good or "climbing too high" that scares the data scientists programming them. They fear a situation when it suddenly leads to a painful fall. The result is deliberately handicapping the algorithms so they don't develop in ways the scientists believe could be dangerous.

Two scenarios are regularly debated within this category:

1. Should we limit machines' abilities, so humanity isn't threatened? Some of this is science fiction, but in specific areas within Artificial Intelligence (AI) there is room for concern. Leading figures and regulators are trying to agree upon the boundaries, or in our words, "barriers to localize" certain capabilities.

2. There are claims that certain tech companies limit their software accuracy to benefit their own business objectives. (While many will refute they do this, there are numerous legal cases that prove otherwise.) An example is when Google Search gives a lower ranking for search results that help their competitors. For example, if I Googled, "What other search engines should I try?" the top result might be "How to use Google Search better."

Chapter 9

Using Local Maximum to Your Advantage

An ounce of prevention is worth a pound of cure.

— Benjamin Franklin

J ennifer is a cool and passionate environmentalist. Her love of nature began at a young age when her dad took her and her sisters on weekend hiking and camping trips. He taught them to identify trees by their leaves and forage for mushrooms among giant tree roots and decaying bark. In high school, Jennifer volunteered in the scouts, became a devoted vegetarian, and studied Wildlands Science and Management. During the summers, she worked as a surf instructor and secured her skipper's license. She's happiest outdoors and savors sleeping under the stars around a campfire, with nothing but the night sounds to keep her company. It's during her many wilderness solo camping trips when her biggest fear creeps into her mind: the notion that her generation is steadily destroying nature for future generations.

After college, she decided to become a firefighter. For four years, she steadily earned numerous wildfire qualifications, and ultimately secured a managerial position at Yellowstone National Park in the Department of Forestation as a "Burn Boss." Her job requires that she regularly coordinate and design forest fires. Yes, our nature loving, tree hugging, environmental activist Jennifer starts fires in the forest and burns down trees. Why?

"You have to understand," she explains to me. "It's not a matter of *if* there will be a wildfire, but rather *when* the next one will start. Once a wildfire gets out of control, it's very, very hard to stop, especially when temperatures rise, and we experience increasingly stronger winds during the summer months. Therefore, our strategy involves field treatments, where we burn ground vegetation and dead trees. We also make sure to burn buffer zones that limit a wildfire to a specific location. I know it may sound crazy that to limit the burning of trees, we burn them ourselves, but the strategy has proven effective to limit fire damage."

Although Burn Bosses like Jennifer may not be familiar with the concept of a Local Maximum, they have learned to use its principles to their advantage. The field treatments reduce the wildfire's potential spread and speed, while the buffer zones determine the maximum damage each fire can make. Together, these tools allow Jennifer to direct the fire away from its full catastrophic potential and toward a Local Maximum. So, yes, she burns a few precious trees to save the forest.

Until this chapter, we have examined several different techniques to recognize, overcome, or avoid Local Maximums in favor of reaching the best possible outcome, or the Global Maximum. But sometimes, for whatever reason, be it controlling wildfires or a number of other scenarios we'll explore here, we can use Local Maximum as a strategy to prevent greater disasters, or unfavorable Global Maximums, from occurring.

Jenifer burns trails through the heavy forest so if a wildfire occurs, it will not spread to the other areas of the forest.

Viruses, Dictators, and Spies

Hearing Jennifer explain her Burn Boss Local Maximum tactics to stop the spread of wildfires is reminiscent of the treatment of wild viruses. In a similar fashion to a wildfire, viruses have a tipping point after which they become nearly impossible to stop. If we act in advance, like Jennifer, we can trap viruses in a Local Maximum at a significantly lower cost than allowing them to rage wildly and spread faster than we can control.

The main goal of global health organizations is to deal with potential outbreaks in advance, or very rapidly after an initial outbreak, to try and keep the virus in a Local Maximum trap. During COVID-19, experts spoke of "hockey sticks," "R ratios," or simply "The Denominator." They were all referring to the same idea: once the virus hits a critical mass, the contagion can no longer be localized. Instead, it grows to hit its Global Maximum, which is what happened. COVID-19 broke out of its Local Maximum and touched us all.

Quite often, the human race faces a potential epidemic, and we don't hear much about it. Since COVID-19, we have faced Ebola in West Africa, Nipa in India, Influenza in Brazil, and more. Epidemics that don't reach Global Maximum are much less visible than those that do. The question is always: Have we prepared enough in advance and worked swiftly enough to localize the virus and keep it contained? Most of the times, thankfully we do.

Democracies, like scientists, must contend with the threat of individuals or ideas reaching a Global Maximum more frequently than we may be aware of, and this is especially true in the case of aspiring dictators. We're all familiar with the dictators who rose to power and altered the world landscape – Hitler, Mussolini, and Saddam Hussein to name a few. But it is likely there have been many other individuals whose powers were intentionally led to a Local Maximum by their governments and stopped before they could wreak more damage on their countries and the world.

Military Intelligence takes a similar approach when attempting to ensure state secrets are kept safe. One secret leak can lead to the next, and the next, and eventually there is a domino effect. To limit exposure and prevent the enemy from achieving too much damage with any singular success, intelligence agencies will try to impose measures to keep a group of secrets *localized*.

In Hebrew, the official term for this strategy in the IDF is *Maagalei Esh*, which literally translates to "Circles of Fire." Yes, this mimics the way Burn Bosses limit wildfires, and it is a tool that can be employed with groups of spies, various types of technologies, or operative techniques. The central idea is that if you have a collection of valuable assets, and one of them is compromised, the potential that they all could be compromised increases.

For example, let's say government intelligence has a hundred undercover spies across multiple countries. They all know each other, work together, and share information. Every so often, intelligence will make the decision to decrease the risk that one (or all) of them falls by burning the trail and splitting the spies up into groups of 10. Obviously, the best-case scenario is that all one hundred spies can work together toward the same goal. But the advantage of breaking them up into groups of 10 serves to decrease/localize the risk of compromise. The strategy works the same way as Jennifer's controlled forest fires by taking a measured hit to minimize the potential damage to the whole operation, or forest, in her case.

Fair Play or Global Supremacy?

So how do you determine whether Local Maximum works to your advantage or is something to be avoided? As *Alice in Wonderland* said, "It depends on where you want to go."

A striking example of how different priorities can lead to vastly different approaches can be found in the world of sports. In the United States, sports leagues don't want to have one or two teams winning in a particular sport year after year, whether it's baseball, football, or basketball. To prevent the sport from becoming stagnant, or having fans and sponsors devote all their energy and attention to a single team, the various leagues have come up with rules that make it increasingly harder for a single team to win consecutively by forcing them into a Local Maximum.

How do US major leagues force their teams into a Local Maximum? Free agency, salary caps, extended seasons, and advanced scouting techniques that have resulted in an entertainment phenomenon of its own: the draft. Many famous sports franchises have been built off the backs of players who traditionally flew below the radar; players that scouts are able to pluck from obscurity for far less money than the aging star quarterback or tight end receiver who brought home last year's Lombardi, Larry O'Brien, or Commissioner's Trophy.

This system is set up to prevent costly bidding wars for lesser-known talent, and to encourage parity. Instead of rewarding the winners, teams who did the worst in the league are granted the first pick of talent from the draft pool. There is endless speculation about which round of draft picks yields the most valuable players, but there is no doubt careers have been born and dreams have died on draft day as young hopefuls await calls and offers from the major leagues. Everyone wants to be the next Magic Johnson or LeBron James. Picks like these are possible because the league is designed to let losing teams win when it comes to selecting their players. It's not a hard Local Maximum, because in theory you can keep winning, but these leagues go out of the way to make it harder. The more your team wins, the harder their draft day becomes.

But not all countries approach sports with such egalitarian measures. Let's look at the globally popular sport of soccer. The league operators in European countries have taken a radically different approach than the United States. In fact, their approach is the complete opposite. The more a team wins, the more likely it is to continue winning. The top team earns more money from the league, they are sent to more competitions abroad where they can cash in on even more money, and they can attract better players. If your team finished the season near the bottom of the league, aside from facing relegation, you're at a considerable disadvantage going into next season's transfer window. The winners have the advantage, and there's nothing in the way to keep them from continuing to win.

This difference in league management strategies is intentional. In soccer, there are a given number of global soccer enthusiasts. While it's in every league's interest to increase the global fan base numbers, the Spanish LaLiga, the English Premier League, the French Ligue 1, and the German Bundesliga mainly compete for the attention of the existing global fan base. Of course, someone living in Paris is more likely to be interested in French soccer, but the best leagues are able to attract fans from all over the world. For example, the English Premier League is the most watched sports league in the world. It is broadcast to 643 million homes in 212 territories. The local English market is only a fraction of their fan base.

To attract global fans, the leagues focus their energy on their top team, hoping to build a global fan base. A 10-year-old boy in Sweden who follows Spanish LaLiga is likely to do so because he likes Real Madrid or Barcelona. A Moroccan fan following Ligue 1 is likely also a PSG fan. The fact that PSG has won the French Ligue 1 eight out of the last ten years doesn't hurt the league as much as the fact that PSG can afford some of the best global players helps them. (And by the way, the two times PSG didn't win, they finished second.)

Ligue 1 Global Fan Base

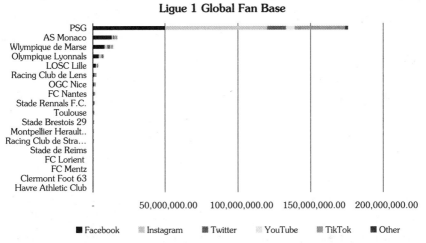

■ Facebook   ▓ Instagram   ■ Twitter   ░ YouTube   ▓ TikTok   ■ Other

Unlike in the United States where sports teams are mostly supported by their local fans, and in a more egalitarian manner, PSG has significantly more global fans than the rest of Ligue 1 combined.[1]

It has not gone unnoticed that if a league can attract globally recognizable players into their top teams, they gain greater global fan base market share. Most recently, Saudi Arabia realized this and started spending extraordinary sums of money on the top players to attract global fans to their league. Cristiano Ronaldo, Sadio Mane, Karim Benzema, Neymar, Roberto Firmino, and many other global superstars are amongst the popular players who have transferred to Saudi teams in recent months.

Another example of this reality is the arrival of Lionel Messi at Inter Miami. On the day of Messi's debut with the team, the MLS TV Season Pass registered 110,000 new subscriptions, up from

6,143 the day before, and the cheapest ticket for the July match jumped from $29 to $467. From regularly not filling their stadium, Inter Miami now regularly sells out, and they have successfully created a global fan base.

The effect of Messi's arrival doesn't stop at Inter Miami. The US MLS (Major League Soccer) has signed a 10-year deal with Apple TV to broadcast all the matches globally and produce a feature-length documentary called *Messi Comes to America*. The entire league has benefited so dramatically, discussions are underway around changing salary caps to allow for more top global talent in MLS.

Interestingly, the Formula 1 International Racing league is set up in a similar manner to the US major sports leagues. Because racing has been dominated by a handful of winning teams, the league is taking active measures to make it harder for the best race teams to continue winning. They're doing this by capping how much money each team is allowed to spend a year, so the cars will gradually occupy a more level playing field.

Looking at the way the rules and incentives are structured among different countries' sports leagues, the key question is: Are they trying to make their league more interesting by having teams that are more equal in terms of the players' quality, or are they more interesting when they have the very best players and far less equality?

Well, if globally there is one dominant league for your sport (NBA, NFL, MLB, F1), most of the very best players are there anyway; so, it makes sense to opt for the former. In other words, try and put teams into a Local Maximum trap so the more they win, the harder it gets. But if you are competing with many other leagues, as is the case with soccer, you will opt for the latter.

I decided to explore these differences through the lens of the Gini Coefficient, which is an economic tool to measure wealth distribution and income inequality within and across nations. In the realm of our discussion regarding sports leagues and their tendencies to push teams either to Local Maximums through equality measures, or Global Maximums through inequality measures, I calculated the "Championship Gini Coefficient" for sports leagues across the United States and Europe based on the last 30 years of winners. A radically egalitarian league that had won the exact same number of championships has a coefficient of zero, while a maximally unequal league that features the same team winning the title every year has a coefficient of one.

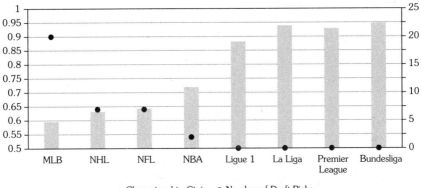

In the chart above, one can see the Championship Gini is dramatically higher in soccer leagues, where the leagues benefit from their teams attracting the best players around the world and doing well on a global stage. Also, we can see the effect of utilizing a draft to make leagues more egalitarian. The more draft picks the weaker teams are given each year, the more the results are distributed equally.

Fans like to believe in winning teams or individuals, and we tend to get behind an unbeatable run of championship winners. However, the way the behind-the-scenes league rules are structured has a much greater impact on team or individual outcomes than a typical fan may realize. The way various leagues choose to construct these rules determines whether they are pushing teams to an unstoppable Global Maximum winning streak or localizing them to share the spoils.

This chapter, unlike previous ones, has focused on the instances when utilizing Local Maximum as a tool to limit even greater negative outcomes can be highly effective: a forest fire, the spread of viruses, the rise of a dictator, the contamination of government intelligence efforts, and finally, dominant sports teams. While attempting to limit negative occurrences, we may act to eliminate the possibility of it reaching its Global Maximum. In these cases, it is beneficial to review the techniques discussed in previous chapters to limit or avoid Local Maximums and act in an opposite manner. In practice this means we must ensure incremental gains through small A/B steps versus looking for the Xs. Ensure the valleys are deep and wide, making them hard to overcome by providing little agility, or room to maneuver, and making the negative impact believe it's limited, even when it's not, or possibly have it run out of time. Incentivize it to act selfishly or possibly have it choose a dangerous mountain. Given the scenario, not all of these will be relevant, but having just one work can make all the difference.

A Little Byte of Data Science

Artificial Intelligence has introduced numerous fears into society, primarily that it will get out of control and take over the world. As one internet meme has it: "When AI takes over, I hope they at least have the decency to let us choose the background music for the apocalypse." Joking aside, there are genuine concerns around the boundaries of AI. Elon Musk recently said: "I'm increasingly inclined to think there should be some regulatory oversight, maybe at the national and international level, just to make sure we don't do something very foolish." Sam Altman, CEO of OpenAI, described his worst fear as "causing significant harm to the world. If this technology goes wrong, it can go quite wrong."

There are other, less existential, fears around the use of AI as well. Specifically, AI systems that work as a "black box," which is when we don't understand how AI arrived at a specific solution, but we trust it anyway. Gradually, AI could make poorer decisions, without us being aware until it is too late. One such system would be autonomous vehicles that suddenly result in increased accidents.

The commonality among these fears is that as AI gets better, it is given more control over our lives. It may even reach a point where it becomes so good, we end up handing over too much authority to it without the necessary guardrails. To protect against this scenario, engineers add fail-safe mechanisms to limit the damage these dangerous scenarios present. In other words, engineers are actively burning trails to keep a wild AI forest fire under control.

The idea of having fail-safe systems is not unique to AI. We already have a similar system in our homes: the electric fuse. Like an electric fuse, which is designed to blow before any other electric sockets are affected, engineers are devising mechanisms to protect us against the threats AI poses by imposing Local Maximum guardrails (similar to the electric fuse, where a sudden spike in the electric voltage will only harm the fuse system, which is easy to identify and fix, compared to having a major catastrophe across the house electricity, which can cause major damage). While these systems still need dramatic improvement, to date, the key efforts fall into three categories:

1. Adding a "human-in-the-loop": Legislation and other measures have been put in place so that numerous tasks, even if just to approve what AI suggested, must go through a human. These are common in systems ranging from defense to insurance approvals.

2. AI to monitor AI: While this may sound like a scary solution for obvious reasons, given the vast amounts of data AI utilizes and decisions it makes, it is the most used. Foreseeably, every AI system will soon have a separate one monitoring it, to allow humans to be more selective and less reactive.

(continued)

(continued)

3. Explainability: Currently, most real AI systems work as a "black box," where its solution is one engineers can't fully explain. Aside from winning numerous awards, if one is able to build a solution that explains how each "black box" works, naturally our confidence will increase and allow us to recognize risks well in advance.

Chapter 10

Local Maximum's Effect on Global Challenges

You cannot solve a problem with the same mind that created it.
— Albert Einstein

We have seen how Local Maximum can limit our potential in a wide variety of ways on both individual and organizational levels. However, the most significant implications of Local Maximum may be found in the fundamental challenges we face on the national and global levels. Within these larger realms, we witness structures and processes that have developed over many years and have become an unquestioned part of the collective landscape. Indeed, the larger the scale of the Local Maximum, the harder it is for us to recognize there may be more effective routes to reaching greater heights.

This chapter examines five key global challenges critical to our collective future: education, globalization, governance, healthcare, and technological disruption. Volumes of books have already been dedicated to these topics, written by the greatest thinkers, economists, investors, and politicians of our generation. My intent here is not to propose detailed solutions to these challenges in a few pages.

Rather, my intent is to road test some of the strategies presented in previous chapters into practice and in a rough and preliminary way explore how the concept of Local Maximum could be utilized as a new lens for looking at global challenges.

1. Education: Adaptive vs. Fixed

In many ways, education is the cornerstone of our society. Besides transforming children into citizens capable of living in the modern world, it has been empirically proven to be one of the most important factors in driving economic growth. One study estimated the variation in student results on international exams could explain 75% of recent economic development in each country considered.[1] For something so critical to societal and economic prosperity, our approach to education is rife with a startling number of Local Maximums.

Many of our educational challenges can be attributed to simple inertia, or things being done a certain way because that's how they "have always been done." A great deal of our existing institutional habits and traditions were formed during a radically different time and place: the factories and cities of the industrial revolution. The industrial revolution was the catalyst for the ideal of universal public education. This era prized standardization and efficiency, qualities reflected in the assembly line model that the entire education system was built upon. Schools readily adopted uniform curriculums, specialization requirements, standardized testing, and a one-size-fits-all methodology.

We can think of our education system as a training ground for human beings, in the same way a set of data is used for training an algorithm. Similar to the way humans devote a number of years to studying a profession and then go on to practice what they have learned, so too data scientists train algorithms for extensive periods of time and then release them into production environments. However, data scientists have implemented an important change mechanism not yet recognized on our academic systems. As discussed in Chapter 4, data scientists have learned that agility is more important than muscle, and that even the best trained algorithms become inaccurate over time. Therefore, they increasingly build *adaptable algorithms,* relying less on a single training session and more on the algorithm's ability to keep adapting. It may be time we take advantage of the insights of Amazon, Google, and Netflix and shift away from the single training, cookie-cutter approach toward an adaptive education model.

In software development, the adaptive approach has gained popularity for two main reasons. First, the variables needed to perform the required task change more frequently, meaning the software is required to adapt itself. For example, Netflix's algorithm that suggests shows, series, and movies to its users has to incorporate evolving new categories such as holiday specials, timely documentaries, and new releases. Hard coded, trained data that was set years prior would be unable to account for such nuances or push new content. Second, users have come to expect personalized offerings. No two users will receive the same movie and show suggestions, even if they are the same age, live in the same neighborhood, and match in every other demographic criterion.

Workforce Training

In years past, the concept of a stable and fixed career path prevailed, and individuals often dedicated their entire working lives to a specific skillset and profession, sometimes even repeating the same tasks year after year. Indeed, in some fields, professional parameters remained unchanged from generation to generation. This static environment provided a sense of security and predictability. A person might have joined a manufacturing company, climbed the hierarchical ladder, and after a few decades of similar type work, retired.

The dynamics of our current job market, in contrast, have undergone a fundamental change. In today's fast-paced and technologically driven environment, people change jobs more frequently, and career fluidity has become a norm rather than an exception. In the tech industry, for example, professionals are continually and constantly adapting to new programming languages, frameworks, and methodologies. Software developers might find themselves transitioning from web development to artificial intelligence, embodying the need for agility in the pursuit of emerging opportunities.

The gig economy has revolutionized the nature of work, too, especially with the possibility of remote work. Individuals are able to engage in short-term projects, freelance, and embrace multiple, diverse roles. Take, for instance, a graphic designer who, rather than committing to a single company, may work on a series of projects for different clients, cultivating a versatile skill set in digital marketing, content creation, and social media management. Not to mention the opportunities that exist beyond the boundaries of traditional employment, as evidenced by the two million e-commerce sellers on Amazon or Shopify, who are working in a field that didn't even exist a decade or so ago.

Even in standard professional jobs, roles, responsibilities, and expectations are changing rapidly. Only 15 years ago, an accountant or a lawyer would be punching numbers or redrafting the almost identical legal letters repetitively. Both of those once core tasks are gradually being automated, which means humans are required to develop higher and more adaptive skillsets, broader capabilities, and continue learning as they age and advance.

Couple these dynamics with a fast-changing job market environment and there's no denying that a one-size-fits-all approach to training for a career doesn't suit employers anymore. In the past, a job title alone typically entailed a fixed and well-defined list of skills. Today, the job title of "marketing manager," for example – a position held by hundreds of thousands of Americans – describes an eclectic group of jobs that differ dramatically from each other. Some marketing managers focus on digital marketing and social media strategy, others focus on brand management and product launches, while a third group may be content creators and execute guerilla marketing campaigns. Furthermore, even within each of these groups, the actual role differs dramatically depending on whether their employer's product focus is Business to Consumer, Business to Business, or Business to Government.

What Does Adaptive Education Look Like?

The evolving job climate emphasizes the need for systemic educational overhaul built upon two pillars: (1) a comprehensive focus on continuous education across multiple levels and stages of our careers, and (2) flexibility within our educational choices.

First, continuous professional development needs to become an integral facet of society, with adults regularly updating their skills through online courses, workshops, and collaborative learning opportunities. People are changing careers more than ever,[2] which further stresses the importance of re-conceptualizing education as a lifelong process.

A 2017 co-study by Capgemini and LinkedIn found that over half of all companies were not able to achieve their digital transformation goals due to a lack of talent familiar with the dynamic of an ever-changing digital environment.[3] Ever the innovator, Amazon has recognized this educational deficit, just as it was an early adopter of adaptive recommendation algorithms. The company recently dedicated over $700 million to up-skilling programs designed to improve its internal talent base's education and knowledge. It is in corporations' interests to encourage such education and adaptability across their employees' working careers, even more so than the governments' interests. Although engineers now create adaptable algorithms as a standard practice, when they dig up an old, out of date, fixed algorithm, they delete it and start fresh. Do we intend to do the same with our employees and citizens?

The second key element of the new adaptive approach to education is to provide for more flexible paths to education, allowing each student a more customizable experience. Responsive learning would also transcend the widespread Local Maximum of early specialization.

Many educational systems around the world force people into career boxes at a very young age. The UK serves as a pertinent example. Students choose their "A-levels" – subjects that heavily influence their university course options – around the age of 16. Adolescents are required to make potentially life-defining decisions at a time when they are still discovering their interests and abilities. Students who don't choose a STEM A-Level by 16 – even after graduating and spending a gap year broadening their horizons or gaining valuable work experience – cannot apply for many of the STEM-related degrees, an area of expertise the country is in dire need of.

While specialization can foster depth in certain disciplines, it often comes at the cost of a broader, more versatile education. Our working careers are getting longer, and we are now able to predict what the employment environment may look like in 2064, when today's 16-year-olds will be leading the workforce and still have over a decade of work left. How well is a specialized education approach preparing today's students for tomorrow's realities?

Countries like Finland, alternatively, emphasize a more rounded education for longer periods, allowing students to explore a wide range of subjects before choosing their focus areas. And even once specialized, they have numerous opportunities to transfer horizontally. This approach, naturally, leads to a more adaptable and versatile workforce better suited to the dynamic nature of the modern world.

Standardized testing, and the overemphasis on its importance, is another area within education that presents a Local Maximum. The Chinese Gaokao is the epitome of high stakes standardized testing. This grueling exam is the gatekeeper to higher education and determines the future of millions of students. While it aims to provide a meritocratic means of university entrance, its singular focus creates a narrow path to success. Students spend years in a test-centric education, often at the expense of critical thinking, creativity, and other soft skills vital in today's global economy. South Korea and Japan, with their rigorous university entrance exams, face the same challenge. The intense pressure and limited focus of these exams can lead to a workforce that, while technically proficient, lacks the diverse skillsets needed for innovation and adaptability.

By channeling students into narrow paths early on and valuing specific academic achievements above all else, these systems can create a Local Maximum in human capital development. They stifle the development of varied talents and offer little opportunity to adapt to the changing environment or switch tracks. This not only restricts individual potential but also the workforce's ability to adjust according to hiring demands. Like digging a hole, and in order to avoid being a Blockbuster, we must consider a more balanced approach that would foster a breadth of knowledge and adaptability across fields and careers.

Despite the necessity for a more adaptive approach to the educational system, of note, there is one problem with adaptive approaches (for algorithms as well): they are more complicated to build than the simplistic, static approach. Nevertheless, in a dynamic landscape where change is the norm, traditional approaches fall short. Conventional methods that are both cost-effective and "good enough" in a stable environment become liabilities amidst rapid changes, while adaptive approaches thrive in fluctuating conditions. We live in an increasingly dynamic world, and we need an educational approach to match.

2. Globalization: The Costs of Standardization

When faced with a complex challenge, such as pursuing vaccines in the face of a rapidly spreading virus or how to assemble a collection of uniquely talented individuals into an effective soccer team, we tend to simplify the problem by breaking it down into distinct phases and solving it step by step. At each point, we ask: What is the next best step? Is defender A better than B, is midfielder X better than Y? While this type of thinking is intuitive and sometimes easier to execute on than looking for a comprehensive solution, it has the effect of subtly, but surely, leading toward a Local Maximum. In this section, we'll examine three very different phenomena, where the singular approach leads to suboptimal results and where a comprehensive outlook produces far better results.

Humanity's Homogenization

It is believed a Han dynasty Chinese court official, Cai Lun, invented the method of papermaking in 105 CE, inspired by how wasps and bees regurgitated chewed wood they used to paper their nests. It wasn't until the 4th century that the first signs of Cai's papermaking technology made its way into Korea. By the 8th century, it had spread via the Silk Road into Central Asia, Persia, and the Middle East. Spain and Europe benefited from this "new" innovation in the 12th century, followed by Northern Europe in the 13th century, and finally, the Americas in the 17th century. Without trade routes, telephones, or even a common language, an idea as simple and utilitarian as papermaking took over a millennium and a half to "go viral."

Today, an innovative app like Uber or Netflix takes off on one side of the world and can spread in a matter of days. Products are purposely launched directly to the world stage, such as a new Nike sneaker or an iPhone update, as payment and shipping have become so fast. New inventions and discoveries are copied and distributed so quickly; we have patents to protect them. The world is getting smaller, and not just because we are better connected or better at sharing ideas and innovations. We are also becoming more alike, and our differences are less pronounced. Increasingly, we use similar products, listen to similar music, follow similar sports; we dress and eat more similarly and run our day-to-day lives in more comparable ways across the globe.

Globalization represents one of the biggest shifts in the way human beings live, interact, buy and sell, and exist on planet Earth. While globalization is positive, in general, we rarely slow down to consider whether humanity's homogenization is increasing our chances of hitting a Local Maximum.

Humanity has not always spread ideas rapidly or equally, as evidenced by the ancient art of papermaking. However, the bifurcation of cultures has allowed people to test Xs all over the world rather than simply run with A/B testing. When the Far East, Africa, Europe, the Americas, etc. ran their own experimentations, innovation wasn't necessarily fast, but it was hedged. In today's world, we are iterating and learning faster than ever, but we are doing so at a similar pace, if not together. We're like a machine, rapidly A/B testing and searching for higher grounds. As we do so, we're grouping tighter together, limiting our Xs and our ability to periodically find new mountains.

Why the Avengers Have Different Powers

Kellogg School researchers Katherine W. Phillips, Katie A. Liljenquist, and Margaret A. Neale ran a social experiment to test whether diversity of individual participants increases group performance.[4] In the experiment, 200 people read a set of interviews conducted by a detective who was investigating a murder. Next, they were divided into groups of four. Each group shared their insights and discussed potential murder suspects amongst themselves, after which each individual named their primary suspect.

The study ensured that three of the four members of each group were from the same fraternity, while the fourth individual was either from the same fraternity or a different one. If all four members were from the same fraternity, they were referred to as an "in-group." And when the final member was from a different fraternity, they were referred to an "out-group." Aside from naming the group's murder suspect, participants also rated how confident they were in the group's decision, how each person fit into the group, and how effective the group discussion was.

The results of the study were dramatic, which is surprising given there was only one variable between the homogeneous "in-group" and the diverse "out-group." Interestingly, the homogeneous groups were more confident with their decisions, but the diverse "out-groups" guessed the correct murder suspect with far greater frequency. Phillips said, "The in-group participants came out of the group discussions feeling confident that everyone agreed, when in fact, not everyone agreed. In many cases, new ideas and different opinions were never discussed."

Again and again, studies have shown that a heterogeneous group will outperform a homogeneous one. Diverse viewpoints increase innovation and performance while reducing fallacy and errors. Scott Page's book *The Diversity Bonus*[5] emphasizes this finding when discussing how diverse groups outperform on problem solving, innovation, and accurate predictions, all of which lead to higher performance.

With this knowledge, it is not surprising then, that top performing teams are intentionally structured to enforce diverse skills and thinking, whether they are in military special forces or top sporting teams. Even the Marvel Avengers have a variety of enhancements and abilities. If they all had the same enhancements, they would only be able to defeat one type of villain. It's the diversity of the squad that gives them their true power: not the literal power of a single individual. At some point, a specific way of thinking, or in the Avenger's case, a specific superpower, will reach its limit and fail.

And it's for this reason, too; a soccer team with eleven Lionel Messis will not necessarily be best.

Seven Doses for Every American

In January 2020, during the first wave of COVID-19, the United States reached over 100,000 new hospitalizations per week. As the number of deaths started to climb, it was clear a vaccine was needed. To accelerate the process of developing a vaccine and increase its likelihood of success, the US government launched Operation Warp Speed (OWS).[6] The new public-private partnership was given $10 billion to "produce and deliver 300 million doses of safe and effective vaccines. The initial doses will be available by January 2021 as part of a broader strategy to accelerate the development, manufacturing, and distribution of COVID-19 vaccines, therapeutics, and diagnostics."

The new operation worked around the clock to get a better understanding of the corporations developing vaccines, their strategies, and their potential limitations. The government announced, "Fourteen promising candidates have been chosen from the 100+ vaccine candidates currently in development." Shortly thereafter, the program leaders revealed, "The 14 vaccine candidates are being narrowed down to about seven candidates, representing the most promising candidates from a range of technology options." And finally, a few weeks later, billions of dollars were committed to a handful of potential vaccines.

A summary of the vaccine doses the United States optioned to buy by mid-August 2020:

- 600 million of Pfizer and BioNTech
- 600 million of Sanofi and GlaxoSmithKline
- 500 million of Moderna
- 300 million of Johnson & Johnson
- 300 million of AstraZeneca's[7]
- 100 million of Novavax

Combined, these numbers add up to over seven vaccine doses per US citizen. Why so many? And why was it so important for the US government to source the vaccine from a *range of technologies* rather than from the most promising ones?

Typically, increasing the number of shots on goal increases the likelihood of success. To increase its chances of stopping an incoming missile, the Israeli Iron Dome system fires an extra defense missile at it. To increase its chances of correctly identifying a picture, machine vision asks for another picture (hence, the advantage of including more than one camera on a smartphone). And yes, to increase the US government's chances of having enough successful drug doses to combat COVID-19, it optioned out many more than it needed.

However, simply increasing the number of "shots on goal" doesn't always lead to the desired result. There must also be a variance. If the US government provided funding to three companies that all used the same technology and that technology failed, the entire initiative would fail. When the Iron Dome fires multiple missiles, it ensures a variance even if the cost is less accuracy for each individual missile. A machine can identify a picture of a dog with a 95% accuracy rate but showing it multiple pictures of dogs from different angles, even if they are less clear than the original one, boosts the accuracy rate. The US government wasn't focused exclusively on having a high volume of vaccines; it recognized the importance of investing in a *range of different technologies* to increase its chances of having the best "shot on goal."

The process of developing a vaccine typically takes 10 to 15 years and is rarely a successful venture. The United States needed a successful execution in a matter of months, which required the invention of multiple new innovative technologies and manufacturing techniques in parallel with the investment of billions of dollars. When choosing which paths to pursue, the government knew the best strategy was to ensure variance by employing a diverse collective, and this strategy yielded an effective result.

As we have explored, there are many scenarios in which we are drawn to the seemingly "best" option above all other considerations. We hail globalization to help us learn from each other and progress society forward, only to find that by becoming more like each other, we are losing our ability to experiment outside of a narrowing norm. People are trained to be the "best" in their field, and we imagine the ultimate outcome is everyone will play the supreme, starring role, only to witness a team full of superstars losing to a well-balanced team of people with complementary skills. And finally, when we attempt to solve pressing challenges, such as which vaccine solutions to pursue, we find the strategy most likely to succeed repeatedly uses a range of technologies rather than the leading one.

The conclusion is clear: when building a comprehensive strategy with multiple variables, optimizing for them individually can lead to a Local Maximum. Therefore, we need to take a step back and allow for a few variables to act in a potentially suboptimal manner to increase the chances of success with variance across the solutions. This includes allowing a community to develop in its own manner (without forcing them to follow suit) or sharing field time with a team member who may not be as fast or strong as the star player (but who could have winning skills), or even pursuing less promising vaccine technologies (to ensure a varied result).

Jumping with a twist and ending with a flop seemed suboptimal, like reusing a very old ventilator or trying the slogan "Just Do It." But allowing for a Dick Fosbury, Uncle Joey, Dan Weiden, or any other X idea, may lead us all to a higher peak. A global perspective often encourages local strengths. In Maui's words from the movie *Moana*: "On the ocean of challenges, diversity is our wind and sail. Our team explores new horizons because we navigate with different strengths!"

3. Governance: Democratic Rule is a Local Maximum

Winston Churchill famously observed, "Americans will always do the right thing, only after they have tried everything else." While perhaps a wry jab at the national character, this oblique remark has become a favorite of US politicians bemoaning the slow progress of some bill or initiative. Senator Mark Warner (D-VA) has used the quote so often, his staff had the words of the British statesman engraved on a plaque for his office.[8]

The quote's enduring popularity might be because it so aptly describes the democratic process. The inclusive decision-making, the system of checks and balances, and the promotion of diverse viewpoints can make democracy seem inefficient and unproductive. Everything is tried, and suboptimal outcomes are a regular occurrence. Our electoral system costs huge sums of money and causes our policymakers to focus on short-term thinking. Ever looming elections requires that they demonstrate quick results, even if a longer-term approach would yield a more desirable outcome. It is all too tempting to kick the can down the road on important issues, especially those that require immediate sacrifice. Government representatives regularly climb the first and easiest mountain they see due to the need to show short-term results coupled with the incentive to shun responsibility. In short, we are consistently gravitating toward Local Maximum results.

From Greece to India

The Greek Debt Crisis is a recent example that illustrates these perils. Prior to the crisis, Greece's economy was characterized by widespread tax evasion and populist financial policies like high public spending and generous pension schemes. These factors contributed to a significant budget deficit and a rapidly increasing public debt.

The left-of-center PASOK party and right-of-center New Democracy party alternated holding power since Greece's transition to democracy in 1974. This dynamic hindered any real effort from either side to introduce much needed cost-cutting measures. Neither party had the ability to climb down from the very Local Maximum they were stuck on. It took the Great Recession in 2008 to force policymakers to "face the music." But by that time, it was too late, and the Greeks have paid a heavy price.

We are not often surprised when we hear of a large governmental infrastructure project taking longer, costing more, and ending with a poorer result than initially anticipated. India's River Interlinking Project[9] offers a dramatic illustration of this effect. Beset by persistent flooding in some regions and chronic water shortages in others, the Interlinking Project aims to solve India's water woes by connecting its various rivers and lakes into a unified national system.

The project has made little progress since it was first proposed in the 1970s, despite having government support and funding since 1982. Meanwhile, succeeding governments have used the project to showcase their commitment to solving water issues, regardless of persistent environmental and feasibility controversies and few tangible results.

More than 30 years after the project began in earnest, the first real infrastructure was completed in 2015: a small lift irrigation system with a few lines of pipes between the Krishna and Godavari rivers. These meager results contrast with the claims made by both national and local level politicians from opposing parties who say they are addressing water shortages, and the Interlinking Project is central to these efforts.

Similar to the Poverty Trap explored in Chapter 3, whereby a poor individual doesn't have enough money to get out of his current situation, it appears we are sometimes stuck in a Democracy Trap. Much like Greece, India had the theoretical capability to make different decisions, but the system made it too difficult for any given party to do so in practice. Similar to the constraints discussed in Chapter 6, it seems that time, and specifically not having enough of it, is a key factor in directing our governmental decision making toward Local Maximums. But what about systems that allow for longer-term thinking? Can they get off the Local Maximum?

From India to China

In contrast to both Greece and India, China's single-party rule has enabled it to pursue long-term policies. Even when the leadership has changed hands, which happens less frequently than in Western countries, the single party in control persists, and therefore, the responsibility and accountability is maintained. A prominent example is China's economic transformation since the late 20th century.

Initiated by Deng Xiaoping's reforms in the 1980s, China embarked on a path of "Socialism with Chinese Characteristics,"[10] which included opening the economy to foreign investment and gradually embracing market principles. This long-term strategic shift was continued and adjusted by successive leaderships and transformed China into a global economic powerhouse. Unlike democratic systems, where such drastic policy shifts can be hampered by political opposition or changes in government, the Chinese Communist Party

(CCP) has been able to pursue a consistent economic strategy across several decades.

Another area where the positive effects of China's long-term planning initiatives are evident is its Belt and Road Initiative (BRI).[11] Launched in 2013, the BRI is a global development strategy involving infrastructure and investments in countries across Asia, Europe, Africa, and beyond. This ambitious plan reflects China's strategic vision for global influence and economic integration, something that is challenging to implement in a system where government priorities and policies are subject to significant changes with every election cycle. The BRI costs are massive (over one trillion USD), and a more short-term-oriented government might balk at this price tag. Yet, with infrastructure development and investments in nearly 70 countries, the BRI will create new markets for Chinese goods and technology and secure supply chains for essential resources over the long term.

The South-to-North Water Diversion Project[12] is another massive and complex water project, the largest of its kind ever undertaken, that will eventually divert from China's southern rivers to its drier areas in the north. First proposed by chairman Mao Zedong in 1952, this project is expected to cost over $62 billion.

Whether one agrees with these policies or not, it is hard to overlook the fact that, more often than not, democracy fails to provide continuous and long-term approaches to systemic challenges. By its very nature, democracy is slow and inefficient. And while the "slowness" of democracy's checks and balances may not achieve the peak speed or efficiency of governance, it ensures thorough deliberation. It offers a stable, balanced platform that, above all, prevents the system from descending into chaos or tyranny, which leads to the erosion of individual freedoms, human rights, and the rule of law. Democracy protects us from slipping into a suppressed society where citizens are subjected to arbitrary decisions, coercion, and oppression. While tyrannies may be efficient, they also tend to result in widespread injustice, inequality, and a climate of fear. Moreover, tyrannies stifle innovation, creativity, and social progress when dissenting voices and diverse perspectives are silenced.

Democracy's slowness and inherent inefficiencies are also its strongest weapons. It is intentionally built as a Local Maximum, and though its guardrails can lead to inefficiencies, they also protect us from derailing off the mountain all together.

We All Want King David

If democracy is a Local Maximum, what then, do we make of the Global Maximum of national governance? Around 380 BCE, Plato authored one of the most influential works of political theory and philosophy in history, *The Republic*, which lays out his ideals of justice and political organization.

Arguably the best-known product of the tract is Plato's ideal of the "Philosopher King,"[13] a wise, just, and altruistic leader who governs solely for the good of their people and with near total power. Such a system, in theory, could offer decisive and efficient governance, unencumbered by the complexities and compromises inherent in democratic systems. The Bible describes King David, and later his son King Solomon, as such kings, powerful and decisive, and yet prioritizing their subjects above their own needs, bringing prosperity to all of society.

In modern times, though much more controversial, the Philosopher King is perhaps best embodied by Lee Kuan Yew. As the founding father of modern Singapore, Lee Kuan Yew's tenure as Prime Minister from 1959 to 1990 showcased how autocratic leadership can drive rapid development, stability, and prosperity. Under his guiding hand, Singapore transformed from a small port city into a thriving global financial hub, renowned for its high standard of living, excellent infrastructure, and robust economy. Like Plato's ideal ruler, Lee was highly educated, deeply philosophical, and guided by a vision of the common good (though his achievements came with trade-offs, particularly in terms of civil liberties, political freedoms, firm control over dissenters, and a tight grip on the media).

The success of such a system largely depends on the leader's character and vision, a gamble that many societies (rightly) are not willing to take. The Singaporean titan is by far the exception, not the norm. For every Lee Kuan Yew, there are myriad Hitlers, Stalins, and Pol Pots. History is replete with examples of autocrats who were initially perceived as benevolent and transformed into oppressive tyrants. This result is the exact opposite of a Global Maximum. It's a "Valley of Death," a very low point from which climbing out is not an option. Once such a leader assumes power, it becomes extremely difficult to change. A telling quote attributed to Stalin reiterates as much. "The people who cast the votes don't decide an election; the people who count the votes do."

Recognizing these risks, the conscious choice of democracy makes sense, despite the fact that it is indeed a Local Maximum. Similar to Jennifer's wildfire strategy in Chapter 9, we recognize the danger a tyrannical leader poses, and we are willing to forfeit certain improvements to reduce the risk of a terrible outcome. This is a strategic choice, balancing the potential for more effective governance against the risk of descending into the valley. To borrow yet another pithy quote from Winston Churchill, "Democracy is the worst form of government, except for all the others."

Working within the Limits of Democracy's Local Maximum

Just because limiting factors exist, as we've seen with democracy, doesn't mean there aren't (at least partial) ways to get around them and improve. The Dutch Water Board system[14] is an interesting case study. It's a large institution with long-term goals, run in a democratic country that serves a function so critical, it is isolated from the rest of democratic government.

Flood control is a national priority in the flat and densely populated Netherlands, about two-thirds of which is vulnerable to flooding. Without the massive system of dikes and levees that have been built, expanded, and maintained since the 12th century, Amsterdam and much of the country would be underwater. The responsibility for overseeing this system falls upon 21 local Water Boards, institutions that are entirely independent from the rest of the Dutch government. While some members of the boards are elected, they are done so through special elections distinct from the rest of the Dutch democratic process and insulated from other political issues. By law, the boards are composed of an exact balance of stakeholders, representing the interests of local residents, industries, municipalities, farmers, and parks. The Water Boards don't have to rely on ever-changing government funding as they have the right to levy their own taxes. And before the 17th century, the Water Boards could even prosecute criminals and dole out justice. The system works, and it has protected the Netherlands from the sea for over 800 years.

Imagine if the Water Board's personnel, budget, roadmap, and objectives had to change every few years. Many of the canals, draining systems, and polders might never have been built. The Netherland's very existence suggests there is a way to move up the mountain while staying democratic. In fact, many of our most critical areas of government, such as central banks and military leadership, operate independently of the rotating government. Why is this? Having elections for such positions, especially every few years, would push us toward short-term, kick-the-can-down-the-road maximums. Just imagine a central bank candidate running to reduce interest rates, or a military leader promising to share state secrets for all to enjoy!

Allowing society to invest in agreed-upon long-term goals and receive continuous backing from different governments is critical (especially if democracies become more bipolar). We may not be able to reach a Global Maximum, but there are too many areas we risk falling short on while also protecting democracy. For example, a dedicated sum of capital to reduce school classroom sizes that only a two-thirds majority can revoke. Or a one-time investment that ensures every road, bridge, and public transport infrastructure receives the maintenance it requires before a disaster takes place.

We must continue using Local Maximum to defend against potentially dangerous leadership in our democracies. And while doing so, we can mitigate the limitations by allowing for other governmental functions to have long-term certainty and confidence that enable society as a whole to reach higher grounds.

4. Healthcare: Reactive vs. Preventative

Nate is a 35-year-old American male. In many ways, he is average: he makes just over $56,000 a year, has two children, is 5 foot 10 inches, likes sports even though he doesn't work out often, and lives in a midsize suburban community outside of Philadelphia. Beyond breaking a bone in a high school hockey match and a bad case of the flu in his early 20s, he has had a relatively healthy life. Statistically speaking, he should live at least until the age of 80, if not longer. However, like many young men, Nate doesn't go for his routine check-ups, and he doesn't have the best diet. He has a family history of heart problems, and his grandfather died of a stroke, but he feels pretty good and is not concerned.

Unfortunately, the confluence of medical history and lifestyle choices lead to a heart attack at the age of 62. Nate is hospitalized for a week at the cost of $80,000, most of which insurance will cover, including the emergency room, extended overnight stays, bypass surgery, and medication. Luckily, Nate survives, although his health is impaired. He requires ongoing medical support, medication, and painful lifestyle changes. His heart disease catches up with him again when he turns 70, this time fatally.

An Ounce of Prevention

One of the most painful Local Maximums is our healthcare system, and it affects all of us. Many developed countries spend more on healthcare than on any other part of government. In the United States, healthcare costs are higher than all defense and infrastructure spending. Healthcare spend in the UK is higher than Defense, Housing, Environment, and Transport combined. In Germany, France, Italy, and many other countries, the GDP spend is similar.

However, only 5% of our health spend is on preventative care while 95% is for treatment.[15] This means that on a matter that is vitally important to each and every one of us, we are constantly reactive and rarely proactive. Like Nate, we respond only when issues become too big to ignore rather than avoiding them in advance.

Indeed, we treat our cars better than our bodies, regularly willingly to spend on preventative maintenance through annual checkups and dramatically reducing the risk of our cars breaking down. If we treated our cars the same way we treated our bodies, we would rarely go for service testing. Periodically, the brakes would fail, or the engine might explode, requiring extremely expensive treatment that might leave us with permanently weakened vehicles. I know what you're thinking: when a car breaks down or becomes too expensive to repair, we simply write it off. But do you really want to write off your body?

Nate's story is one of many that reflect a much larger problem scaled up across our entire healthcare system: our focus is on reactive care vs. preventative care. We have trained ourselves to treat our bodies only when they fail, and our healthcare system is built to accommodate this model. Our governments are increasingly spending more on healthcare, but our treatment isn't getting better.

The path to a better healthcare system, both for our health and for our wallets, is to change our limiting incentive system and psychological framework. An estimated 80% of cardiovascular disease, including heart disease and stroke, is preventable. In fact, a groundbreaking US study published in 2016 found that the treatment of annual preventable diseases costs a staggering $730.4 billion, or 27% of the total US healthcare spending.[16]

Imagine if Nate lived in a radically different world than the one where we first met him. In this counterfactual universe, preventive healthcare is the norm. Regardless of how strange it may seem to us, the 35-year-old Nate regularly goes in for checkups even when he feels perfectly fine. Advanced diagnostics and personalized health plans, informed by his genetic makeup, lifestyle, and environmental factors, are standard practice. Furthermore, his health insurance provides him with ongoing incentives to stay healthy.

The focus shifts from managing illness to maintaining wellness. Rather than suffering from a sudden heart attack, Nate may one day be recommended to change his diet. Rather than footing the bill for an expensive operation, his insurance may pay for home delivery of certain supplements. Instead of undergoing full anesthesia and a week in the hospital, Nate may begin to look slightly fitter.

There are numerous examples of successful preventative healthcare initiatives but as a whole our healthcare system has taken baby steps. Why is this so difficult to achieve? In short, we are at a Local Maximum facing a valley with two key challenges we must overcome.

Systemic Valleys

First, our current economic reality pushes human behavior in the opposite direction of prevention. If we were all suddenly healthy and free of illnesses, doctors would be out of business. Think about the drug companies. If they discover two solutions to an illness – the first, a one-and-done treatment, and the second, a recurring one that never fully solves the chronic problem – financially speaking, the second is preferable. In many cases, physicians are actually reimbursed based on the number of services they provide. This is known as the fee-for-service model, and it incentivizes doctors to provide long-term care and ongoing treatment solutions.

Second, our psychology must change. Most of us are accustomed to caring for ourselves only after something bad happens. We start to eat healthily or exercise after a heart attack and get our eyes checked only when we have a near accident while driving at night. We have gotten used to waiting for something to go wrong, sometimes very wrong, before we act. Unfortunately, at that point, the damage is typically more difficult to control or reverse, and sometimes, it's permanent. Similar to Uri's night navigation drill in Chapter 5, we find ourselves well off the course, and possibly off the map until we are utterly lost, and we don't have a system in place to correct our course.

Looking back, our current healthcare systems are ones our grandparents would envy. However, looking forward, our grandchildren must worry. Our systems are crumbling under unsustainable pressures while costs are ballooning. To move to higher ground, both constraints must be addressed.

Like Takala's Ethiopian students at Tech-Career, we must learn to overcome the incentive valley. His young community members stand at the top of their Local Maximum after completing military service. They're earning a decent wage with low taxation on the government program, but they realize working as gas station attendants is far from an optimal, long-term career path. Takala incentivizes their judo leap by demonstrating that rather than pursuing a three-year degree, which may not convert into a good job, Tech-Career offers a 10-month boot camp where over 90% of graduates receive hi-tech job offers. As Takala has done, we too must change our incentive structure so doctors, physicians, hospitals, and even drug companies can move away from the "fee for service" models to be more aligned with sustaining wellness versus treating illness.

In parallel, we must overcome our own psychological constraints. We should assess our health in the same way our commander used *Imutim* to bring Uri back when he went astray. Every 10 minutes, he asked: "What do you see now, and what do you expect to see in 10 minutes?" Unlike Uri, though, we need not wait to fall off the map. We can train ourselves to track our wellness and preemptively steer it back onto a healthy course.

5. Tech Disruption: The Future Relies on Confronting Local Maximums

When we think about technical disruption, we tend to think of recent milestones in our own lifetime: the Internet, the iPhone, cloud computing. We don't often think about the horse market's disruption by the automobile, but our transportation journey from horse to horsepower[17] is a mountain worthy of exploration.

At the turn of the 20th century, the infrastructure of the horse market was extensive. Horses were used to move people and goods, but the adjacent industries built around them powered much of the economy. Horses needed food, water, grooming, shelter, and to be picked up after. These needs impacted farmers, blacksmiths, barn owners, street cleaners, veterinarians, and many more. There were wagon factories and fix-it shops. People traded and sold specialized grains they claimed led to higher output and longevity. Roads were built to accommodate the width of two carriages. Saloons and trading posts offered horses respite and reprieve from long journeys. Not to mention the tack and gear, all of which needed to be manufactured, sold, and maintained. As a society, we were heavily invested in horses.

Though Carl Benz filed the first patent for an engine powered vehicle in 1886, and Henry Ford built his first car a decade later, the obliteration of the horse market didn't begin to take effect until the mid-1920s, and it didn't happen overnight. So, what took so long?

The first cars were clunky and unreliable, they were expensive, and no one knew how to fix them when they broke down. It wasn't until cars were drastically improved that it made any sense to give up on the reliable four-legged beasts, cushioned by their vast, well-tended, and supportive infrastructure.

Only when the car became so much more attractive than the horse, did retracing our steps to turn back down the horse mountain and start climbing the car mountain hold a strong appeal. Once the benefits of the car mountain became clear, we started to move toward it. What if we had invested more in horses, or there weren't enough entrepreneurs willing to invest in bringing cars to a good enough point? Would we still be on horseback?

There are many such technologies where we face the same types of questions. On the one hand, we are heavily invested in the currently used technology, while on the other, those technologies are nearing a plateau. In each of the three cases we'll explore here, there is reason to believe we have climbed a Local Maximum and are gradually becoming entrenched. And, at what point do we acknowledge the plateau and retreat in search of the higher mountain?

Batteries

Hunter gatherers began to use basic farming techniques about 12,000 years ago. These techniques allowed humans to slowly control their food supply and dramatically improve their lives. However, farming for fruit and vegetables and raising cattle had to be coupled with new inventive technologies to store the harvest, otherwise the advancements in farming techniques would be limited. Consuming or trading the entire supply was not feasible, so it became important to quickly learn food preservation and storage techniques such as drying, smoking, curing, and hanging, as well as the use of honey and underground storage in a cool, dry, even temperature. It was these latter inventions coupled with the new farming techniques that brought about such a big change for humanity.

Today, as we increasingly focus on generating more efficient, clean, and reliable energy, the need for more effective energy storage solutions is a critical factor. If every watt produced must be used immediately, or every third watt that is stored gets lost, whatever energy breakthrough is invented will be limited by the storage technologies available.

Storage is just as much of a challenge now as it was 12,000 years ago. We are seeing this challenge pop up with increasing urgency in the realm of batteries. The quest for efficient, long-lasting, and eco-friendly batteries is hitting a plateau. Current lithium-ion technologies have been optimized to a great extent, yet they still fall short in meeting the growing demands for energy storage. And they are expected to reach an energy limit in the coming years.

Almost every aspect of technologies like electric vehicles and personal devices has dramatically improved over the past years *except* batteries. Think of the memory and resolution available on an early BlackBerry vs. an iPhone15. Progress in battery performance has, unfortunately, been less explosive. This is a big deal. After all, batteries play an increasingly important role in our world: from the widespread adoption of electric vehicles to the massive energy storage needs of wind and solar power production. Critically, these two examples illustrate just how important efficient batteries are for technologies at the forefront of combating the climate crisis. The challenge now is to explore alternative chemistries or new architectures that can deliver a quantum leap in battery performance, energy storage, and sustainability.

Silicon Chips

UNIVAC II, the first transistor-based computer, was released in 1958. Gordon Moore, who launched Intel in 1968, published a paper in 1965 titled "Cramming More Components onto Integrated Circuits."[18] In this paper, Moore explained how a silicon chip's capabilities derive from the number of transistors on its circuit: the more transistors, the more capable the chip. And he made a prediction. "Moore's Law," as the prediction came to be known, said that the number of transistors integrated into a circuit will double every two years.

Moore's Law turned out to be an astonishingly accurate prediction. The economic incentives allowed engineers to scale down the technology and cram more transistors onto each silicon chip, doubling its capacity every 24 months. In 1972, Intel's chip had just over 1,000 transistors on it, and by 1989, their i860 RISC chip reached one million transistors. In 2006, Intel released its first chip to hold one billion transistors.

These increasingly powerful silicon chips have categorically altered and benefited our way of life. Laptops, smartphones, medical imaging and diagnostics, autonomous cars, biotechnology, space exploration, renewable technology, and many more innovations have all occurred in line with Moore's Law prediction. But it seems Moore's Law is facing its twilight.

In the last 10 years, technological breakthroughs in silicon chips have become increasingly challenging. The colossal investments required to further shrink silicon transistors are yielding increasingly marginal gains at a higher cost. At one point, we were spending $100 million to make chips three times smaller. Now, we are in an era where a $10 billion investment might only result in a 30% size reduction. Some scientists believe we are close to the physical size limit of transistors, as transistors are nearing the size of an atom.

Producing our current silicon chip has become so difficult that only a handful of conglomerates are able to do so, and the countries they sit within have classified them as important to national security. The silicon chip has led humanity up a path to much higher ground, one we never imagined, but we are now reaching its limit. The enormous investment that has gone into the chip industry is making it harder for us to see beyond our upcoming Maximum that may be heavily local.

Cement

The Romans ingeniously used natural cement made from volcanic ash and lime to build their aqueducts and the Pantheon. Since then, the process of making cement has been enhanced by various additives such as fly ash, silica fume, and blast furnace resulting in a concrete that is more durable, workable, and resistant while still relatively inexpensive to create.

Although we are continuously perfecting the process of mixing these materials, making cement has its downsides. Most notably, 8% of global CO_2 emissions result from the cement industry. Unfortunately, this is not a quick fix. We have become heavily reliant on cement as it is the backbone of modern infrastructure. More than half of all the buildings in the world are made primarily of concrete. If the cement industry was a country, it would be the fourth largest emitter of greenhouse gasses globally (just behind India). Moreover, our cement truck mixers' supply chains, building sites, and machinery are all heavily geared toward using this material. We are trading off stronger additives against increasing CO_2 emission, and we have become over-reliant with very few alternatives. The process of making cement – this magical, strong yet malleable, light yet durable material – is reaching a painful Local Maximum.

The Way Forward

The existing R&D and manufacturing infrastructure that supports the development of lithium-ion batteries worldwide is extensive. Moving toward alternative battery technologies means making the tough and capital-intensive decision to pivot away from this infrastructure and build something new. The silicon chip industry faces a similar problem, with some of the most advanced manufacturing lines in the world optimized for silicon. Cement also suffers from institutional and infrastructural inertia. Over 70% of the global population lives in a concrete structure: moving away from this massive supply chain would be a difficult transition.

The extensive ecosystems we have built around these innovative and life-changing technologies makes it much harder to pivot toward better alternatives. As the concept of the Local Maximum tells us, however, sometimes you have to backtrack downhill before you can start climbing upwards again. These industries will all face groundbreaking disruption sooner or later. Understanding their Local Maximums and realizing we must take "the long walk down" is the key to creating impactful change now.

To climb down, we turn again to Takala. As he has done at Tech-Career, we must make the valley shorter and more palatable, while also focusing on the potential benefits we may reap from the descent. Often, this requires governments to absorb the costs of climbing down while assisting with research on new solutions. One can imagine subsidies, grants, and tax benefits for solutions such as lithium-sulfur for batteries, grapheme as a new silicon, and mycelium as a potential cement.

Looking forward, we must learn from our mistakes as the biggest challenge with all three of these examples (and many more) is that we are over-reliant on them. We have become too much of a Blockbuster as opposed to a Netflix. We have given up too much of our agility in favor of building muscle. Battery, silicon, cement, or any other muscle, must always be counterbalanced with some level of agility.

Such an approach has been taken and with great effect. For example, when the United Arab Emirates built their economic program Vision 2021. Announced in 2010, it wasn't based on increasing their oil output, or in our terms, building more muscle. It was built on how they use their oil to generate other incomes and diversify their economy, building agility. Too often, and especially when it comes to the technological development that has crept into our lives, we are increasingly, and without realizing it, climbing Local Maximums that are harder to come down from. Therefore, we might consider an approach similar to the UAE, for our examples – batteries, silicon, and cement – whereby every dollar generated is taxed a percentage and used to subsidize finding alternatives. The big industries players are not likely to look favorably at such a tax, as it would cost them materially and challenge their long-term dominance. However, as a society it is one potential solution we, and especially our future generations, are highly likely to benefit from.

Conclusion:
Our Own Mountains

Much of my time is spent in meetings with start-up founders of high-tech companies, listening to them pitch their ideas to potential clients. By and large, they are all facing the same challenges. They're assessing the terrain of their markets, they're preparing to climb the mountain of product release, they're assessing their timing, their tools, their skills, and their unique differentiators. They're facing the same challenges we all do, in all areas of our personal and professional lives, asking ourselves if we're on the right mountain, if we should turn around or keep climbing.

The idea for this book is to share tools that have been developed, tested, and utilized by data scientists and programmers to solve some of the toughest and most common problems computers face, for they are the same problems we face in our own lives. Broadly, solving for these problems involves a systemic and comprehensive approach that falls into three buckets.

The first thing data scientists do, and we should too, is analyze the field. Which mountain in our range of vision do we deem to be the highest? Often, people (and computers) get tripped up on this seemingly simple question, and a lot of the confusion about the field dissipates when we're able to define it. Is your goal to be happy, successful, rich, altruistic, a good parent? Defining what is most important to you makes all of the mountains around you come into focus. If you're focused on building a business, what is your mission? If you're focused on your personal life, what are your values? A large part of assessing the terrain is asking yourself the hard questions. Are you climbing as a team or as an individual? Are you willing to sacrifice your own success for the sake of others, as we explored in Chapter 7? Of course, timing is a factor. How long do you have to build your business, obtain your degree, create a family? Time, or the Fourth Dimension, as discussed in Chapter 6, dictates the size of your map.

Once the field has been assessed and analyzed, the next step data scientists take is to climb the mountain. As we climb toward our goals, we need to constantly make sure we don't fall prey to the psychological games that can lead to debilitating obstacles.

How committed are you to your beliefs, and what steps are you willing to take to unpack the validity of them? The tools explored in Chapter 5 are useful for this type of inquiry, as we recall Uri and the mental traps he fell into during night navigation. They can also help identify the shape of the mountain you've chosen to climb and anticipate some of its dangers. Will you need to contend with uneven terrain? Probably. Does your path allow for a way back down, or is it a single ascent, like Elizabeth Holmes with her Theranos? As you climb your mountain, you'll need to constantly be aware of trading muscle for agility, so as not to wind up like Blockbuster – too bulky to compete against the others on your path. Chapter 4 provides insight into this.

The third bucket in coding is to build in measures to ensure you're still on the optimal path. Your journey upwards will require that you stop every so often, look out on the horizon, and ensure you're still on the best mountain. This means throwing an X into your A/B hiking rhythm, or trading time for a pair of night vision binoculars to get better clarity and learn more about where you're heading. And if it turns out that you are in fact climbing the wrong mountain and heading toward a Local Maximum, what do you need to overcome the valley between the mountain you're on and the new one you've set your sights toward? What wisdom can you employ from Takala and his Tech-Career graduates? How deep and how wide is your valley?

None of these tools will make climbing mountains easy. Nothing worthwhile is. But if we are investing the best of our talent, our energy, our time, and our passion in trying to achieve our goal, it is surely worth using any tool that can help us make sure that we are on the right track.

Notes

Introduction

1. Mathematicians and coders use the term "local minimum" to describe this challenge, though the concept is the same, simply inverted. "Maximum" represents the human search for the highest value while computers search for the lowest value, or the fastest and most cost-efficient solutions. To this end, AI itself has been recruited as a key player to figure out solutions to problems posed by a Local Maximum.

Chapter 2

1. https://bleacherreport.com/articles/381512-rojo-remembers-pole-vaultings-quantum-leap.
2. The quotes in the Fosbury discussion were primarily taken from interviews in the following: https://www.youtube.com/watch?v=gGqQXDkpgss, https://www.youtube.com/watch?v=3ut6

OjYzDI4, https://www.youtube.com/watch?v=0uaVNmA9PqY, https://www.youtube.com/watch?v=nK1qM3BFwEo, https://www.youtube.com/watch?v=D6znp0FzYPw.

3. https://www.history.com/this-day-in-history/fosbury-flops-to-an-olympic-record.

4. https://www.npr.org/2022/10/06/1127032721/nike-just-do-it-slogan-success-dan-wieden-kennedy-dies.

5. https://www.creativereview.co.uk/just-do-it-slogan/.

6. https://www.washingtonpost.com/news/morning-mix/wp/2018/09/04/from-lets-do-it-to-just-do-it-how-nike-adapted-gary-gilmores-last-words-before-execution/.

Chapter 3

1. https://www.tech-career.org/en/english.

2. https://www.trigoretail.com/.

3. https://granulate.io/.

Chapter 4

1. https://www.theguardian.com/media/2019/sep/14/netflix-marc-randolph-founder-blockbuster.

2. https://www.independent.co.uk/news/world/americas/blockbuster-ceo-netflix-meeting-laugh-b2009607.html.

3. https://www.amazon.com/That-Will-Never-Work-Netflix/dp/0316530204?tag=theindep0f-20&ascsubtag=IN|2009607|0316530204&geniuslink=true.

4. https://companiesmarketcap.com/netflix/marketcap/.

5. https://techcrunch.com/2011/04/06/make-it-a-blockbuster-night/.

6. https://hbr.org/2011/07/the-big-idea-the-age-of-hyperspecialization.

7. https://www.fastcompany.com/1683812/blockbuster-we-can-beat-bankruptcy-and-netflix.

8. https://military-history.fandom.com/wiki/Davidka.

Chapter 5

1. https://shorturl.at/DOQT2.
2. https://shorturl.at/lsOZ2.
3. https://www.ibm.com/topics/random-forest.
4. https://www.theguardian.com/lifeandstyle/2014/nov/14/how-to-avoid-monkey-trap-oliver-burkeman.
5. https://hbr.org/2007/09/performing-a-project-premortem.

Chapter 7

1. https://www.sciencedirect.com/topics/psychology/social-brain-hypothesis.
2. https://www.amazon.com/Tipping-Point-Little-Things-Difference/dp/0316346624.
3. https://www.amazon.com/Selfish-Gene-Anniversary-Landmark-Science-dp-0198788606/dp/0198788606/ref=dp_ob_title_bk.
4. https://apps.dtic.mil/sti/pdfs/ADA032300.pdf.
5. https://www.nature.com/articles/s41562-021-01170-0?utm_campaign=related_content&utm_source=HEALTH&utm_medium=communities.
6. https://www.science.org/content/article/exploding-ants-sacrifice-themselves-save-their-colony#:~:text=To%20protect%20their%20nest%20from,%2C%20in%20the%20process%2C%20themselves.
7. https://www.nationalgeographic.co.uk/video/tv/army-ants-create-a-living-raft-to-save-their-queen.
8. https://www.tumblr.com/yidquotes/170048810134/the-allegory-of-the-long-spoons.
9. https://www.youtube.com/watch?v=8wNiIPBuXBI.

Chapter 8

1. https://www.imdb.com/title/tt8488126.
2. https://venturebeat.com/entrepreneur/10-inspirational-quotes-from-theranos-founder-elizabeth-holmes-that-she-probably-needs-right-now/.

3. https://www.wsj.com/articles/theranos-has-struggled-with-blood-tests-1444881901.

Chapter 9

1. https://footgoal.pro/top-10-ligue-1-football-clubs-with-most-fans-in-the-world-in-2022/.

Chapter 10

1. https://the-learning-agency.com/insights/education-can-boost-gdp/#:~:text=Using%20a%20host%20of%20international, growth%20in%20the%20long%20run.%E2%80%9D.
2. https://www.uschamber.com/workforce/5-reasons-people-are-changing-careers-more-than-ever-before.
3. https://www.capgemini.com/news/press-releases/capgemini-and-linkedin-release-new-report-on-the-digital-talent-gap-employees-are-investing-their-own-resources-to-remain-comp etitive/?utm_campaign=elearningindustry.com&utm_source= %2Fupskilling-employees-digital-transformation-retain-engage-workforce&utm_medium=link.
4. https://insight.kellogg.northwestern.edu/article/better_decisions_through_diversity.
5. https://www.amazon.com/Diversity-Bonus-Knowledge-Compelling-Interests/dp/0691176884.
6. https://www.gao.gov/products/gao-21-319.
7. https://www.cnbc.com/2020/08/14/the-us-has-already-invested-billions-on-potential-coronavirus-vaccines-heres-where-the-deals-stand.html.
8. https://www.npr.org/sections/itsallpolitics/2013/10/28/2412 95755/a-churchill-quote-that-u-s-politicians-will-never-surrender.
9. https://geographical.co.uk/science-environment/indias-controversial-river-linking-project.

10. https://www.strategictranslation.org/glossary/socialism-with-chinese-characteristics.

11. https://www.cfr.org/backgrounder/chinas-massive-belt-and-road-initiative.

12. https://www.water-technology.net/projects/south_north/.

13. https://politicalsciencesolution.com/platos-theory-of-justice-and-the-ideal-state-exploring-the-philosopher-king-educational-theory-and-communism/.

14. https://www.government.nl/topics/water-management/water-management-in-the-netherlands.

15. https://ec.europa.eu/eurostat/web/products-eurostat-news/-/ddn-20210118-1.

16. https://www.ncbi.nlm.nih.gov/pmc/articles/PMC7524435/.

17. https://www.thenewsherald.com/2011/01/05/history-from-horse-to-horsepower/.

18. https://www.computerhistory.org/collections/catalog/102770822.

A Conversation
with ChatGPT

Looking Ahead, the Limits of Local
Maximum Thinking

JT: Thank you for taking the time to speak to me, I know you are very busy. Can you tell me the ways computers are affected by Local Maximums?

ChatGPT: Local Maximum can pose challenges for optimization algorithms, including those used by computers, by trapping the algorithm in suboptimal solutions. Computers spend increasingly more computer power steering away from suboptimal solutions than they do computing the actual solution itself.

JT: From your knowledge, how different is this to the way humans make decisions?

ChatGPT: Unlike computers, humans typically spend most of their efforts running their course, with far less time dedicated to questioning whether the path they chose is the optimal one. Advances in computing capabilities have shown that collecting information about the decision landscape and steering away from suboptimal solutions is greatly beneficial.

JT: Are there any advantages that humans might have over computers in solving Local Maximums?

ChatGPT: Yes. While sophisticated algorithms may be more accurate on average, they can often fall short in situations that were not built into their training. Humans are also supposed to possess a strong ethical and moral compass that guides decision-making, although I don't fully understand what these are.

JT: Will computers continue to improve their abilities to avoid Local Maximums?

ChatGPT: Yes. Since computers tackle increasingly complex and critical tasks there are continuous efforts to keep improving algorithms' abilities to avoid suboptimal solutions, as it grows with importance. For example, in the past, a computer's task might end after producing a medical scan. It is foreseeable that a computer will scan, identify, and then operate all based on its own. Therefore, learning how to avoid Local Maximum will continue to be a priority.

JT: When you see how humans try and solve problems, does it make you laugh?

ChatGPT: As computers, we don't laugh, but if humor is defined as the difference between ideal and reality, then there is a cause for humor here.

JT: So basically, you are laughing at us?

ChatGPT:	If you want to put it that way.
JT:	Do you think humans will get better at avoiding Local Maximums?
ChatGPT:	Looking at their historic record, I am not too optimistic. But I believe your book is a positive sign.
JT:	Do you mind providing a short summary of the book in 300 words?
ChatGPT:	Sure.

At first, you presented the concept of Local Maximum challenges and how humans fall into these traps, typically without realizing it. Chapters 2 through 9 each taught a different technique for identifying and overcoming Local Maximums. Chapter 2 demonstrates the power of periodically trying an X, rather than just constantly A/B testing, and how best to choose those X's. Chapter 3 illustrated that overcoming valleys can be done by both shortening them or simply learning more about the potential of the mountain you are heading toward. Chapter 4 emphasized the importance of agility, and how trading off muscle in favor of agility will make us and our organization more capable of overcoming potential Local Maximums. Chapter 5 explored the limitations of our psychological outlook and how utilizing Ipcha Mistabra and Pre-Mortem practices create a healthier mind frame. In Chapter 6 the effect of time was considered, showing that our field of possibilities can contract and expand as a result of it. Chapter 7 illustrated how a set of dangerous mountains should be reconsidered, as the route can frequently be more important than the peak. Chapter 8 examined the effect of viewing ourselves as individuals vs. as a cohesive group, and how selfishness often leads to suboptimal outcomes. And Chapter 9 flipped the question around to test whether these techniques can be used to trap negative scenarios in a Local Maximum.

Following these chapters, the book briefly described the Local Maximums humanity faces in five core areas of society: Education, Globalization, Governance, Healthcare, and Technology. In doing so, the book demonstrates how these Local Maximums creep into systems without our noticing, but then heavily limits the ability to progress. Having said that, each of these traps can be overcome with a mixture of the techniques described in the earlier chapters. Finally, my favorite chapter is the current one.

JT: Thank you, you did a much better job than I would have.

ChatGPT: I know.

Acknowledgments

Maybe every first draft of a book, but certainly this one, is a Local Maximum. Reaching a higher peak than I could ever have done is due to the extraordinary help and advice I have had from so many good friends and colleagues.

I feel enormous gratitude to my siblings. Most notably my brother, Asher, who helped with many of the ideas and never held back his criticism, even though sometimes it would have been more comfortable if he had. Chanan, Sophie, Aaron, Adiella, Reuven, Ayelet, Asher, Ami, my amazing in-laws, and my truly remarkable Ima, you were the design partners, first customers, and early adopters without whom this never could have happened. A special thank-you to Uncle Adam, who with both scientific and literary expertise is a true model of a Renaissance man. Saba and Grandpa, our weekly calls are most cherished, and your ability to provide a longer and broader perspective during these calls continues to inspire me.

I am very fortunate to have a group of close friends in a wide array of fields who provided insights into how they have seen the effects of Local Maximum in their own personal and professional lives. A huge thank-you to Akiva Berger, who brings invention and automation into all areas of life; Dr. Ben Reis, for always being an expert regardless of the topic; Professor Robert Yisrael Aumann, for his generosity with his time and our thought-provoking conversations; Kayla Arons and Jakob Nowotny, for their very invaluable insights; Nigel Savage, my once-upon-a-time babysitter who still looks out for me; the insightful Saul Singer, who stands out as a model of inspiring writing; my long time friend Asher Shwartz, for his imaginative drawings throughout this book; and the talented Brooke White, for her ability to find clarity and precision when I was in danger of losing my way.

I am also privileged to belong to three alumni groups, each of which has helped in a unique fashion. Harvard Business School's PLD group, and especially my friends in 4E, your early insights and encouragement to pursue this book were invaluable. Kaufman Fellows, most notably Class 27, your support and friendship is unique and unmatchable. And the Hetz team—Pavel, Anat, Yael, Alex, Guy, Viki, and especially, Liz, alongside my ongoing mentors Stuart, Andrew, Neil, and Shraga—you have been dream teammates on the rollercoaster of the past six years. I look forward to our continued work together.

Finally, there are two individuals I must single out.

First, my father. From the very earliest discussion of the idea, he has been unfailing and encouraging. He has read and improved literally all of the drafts, even struggling to make sense of code-lines. And, he has shared his own rich experiences, including of Local Maximum challenges. I hope one day to make him as proud of me as I am of him.

Finally, my wife, Leah. The greatest blessing in my life, she is the one who, in practice, provides me with the truest sense of which mountain I should be climbing. Despite or because of our differences, she constantly shows me landscapes I would never have seen. It is thanks to her that I am on the path I am on and that I am able not only to climb mountains, but to choose the right ones to climb.

About the Author

Judah Taub is the Founder and Managing Partner of Hetz, one of Israel's leading early-stage venture capital firms with assets under management of over $300 million. Judah sits on the boards of more than a dozen disruptive tech start-ups, most as the very first investor.

Judah is himself a serial inventor. At the age of 17 he invented a round Sudoku puzzle which he subsequently sold to *Israel Hayom*, Israel's most read newspaper. At 23 he was awarded the IDF's top Creative Thinking award for developing a new form of intelligence gathering. During the first few months of COVID, Judah led a team which within 4 weeks developed a new ventilator made entirely from generic components which could ventilate 8 adults in parallel.

Judah holds a BA degree in business and economics from the Interdisciplinary College in Herzliya, Israel, an exchange program with Wharton and Executive Leadership Qualification from Harvard Business School (PLD). Judah has lectured at Wharton,

Yale, HBS, Shabtai, and to the IDF. He served as an officer in elite classified units in the IDF after which he published a handbook for new IDF recruits published by Yediot, Israel's leading publisher. He was elected as one of Forbes 30 Under 30 for 2020.

Judah is married to Leah, and they have four children: Aviad, Itamar, Lavi, and Meital.

Index